Thesis for Organization's Culture can impact on Insurance Human Resource Productivity

Babak Nemati

Contents

1-1-Introduction

Today's Insurance Organizations is predominantly dynamic as it poses large opportunities and challenges to the corporate practitioners and policy makers. Understanding such dynamism is very crucial to pursue the Insurance Organizations strategic objectives. There have been researches in literature to explore the effect of Insurance Organizational culture on various human resource development programmes of an Insurance Organizations. For example, scholars including Hofstede, 1980; Ouchi, 1981; Hofstede and Bond, 1988, Kotter and Heskett, 1992; Magee, 2002, claim that Insurance Organizational culture help to provide opportunity and broad structure for the development of human resources' technical and behavioural skills in an Insurance Insurance Organizations. This makes sense because good behavior is driven by ethical values. An Insurance Organizations can guide the conduct of its employees by embedding ethical values in its culture. However, Insurance Organizational excellences could be varied since cultural traits could be source of competitive advantage through casual ambiguity, The world is changing rapidly and the level of Insurance Organizations is also changing due to technological advancements which have affected their human resource developments programs. Moreover, Insurance Organizations differ in their cultural content in terms of the relative ordering of beliefs, values and assumptions.

The HRM function includes a variety of activities, and key among them is deciding on the staffing needs, whether to use independent contractors or hire employees to fill these needs;, recruiting and training the best employees; ensuring that the Insurance Organizations has a team of high performers; dealing with performance issues; and ensuring that personnel and management practices conform to various regulations (McNamara, 2005). HRM also includes managing the Insurance Organizations approach towards employee benefits and compensation, as well as managing employee records and personnel policies (McNamara, 2005). Both Insurance Organizational culture and human resource management work closely together to produce the shared outcome of employee's performance, which determines Insurance Insurance Organizations success (Guest, 1987; Storey, 1992).

Despite the relationship between Insurance Organizations culture, and human resource management as highlighted above, current research and seminar presentation reveals that their relationship is becoming more complex due to the divergent results arising from such studies (Aycan, Kanungo, Mendonca, Deller, Stahl & Kyrshid, 2000). Senyucel (2009) argues that it has become difficult to come up with a commonly acceptable relationship between them. The findings are mostly inconclusive, which suggest further research, either in validating or contributing to the pool of knowledge (Shili, 2008). Hence, the purpose of this research is to examine the relationship between Insurance Organizations culture and human resource management by exploring both direct and indirect cultures. Insurance Organizational culture is not only able to guide behavior and change attitudes within the work environment, but also to give remarkable contributions by influencing behavior and attitudes towards satisfactory performance (Quinn, 1988).

1-2-Problem Statement

Insurance Organizational culture is the topic that recently found his way in the management and Insurance Organizational behavior domain. Demographers, sociologists and psychologists and even economists have recently pay special attention to these new and important topics in management and created lots of researches in identifying the role and importance of these kinds of theories and using them to solve management problems . A group of management scholars doing a study to show that the Insurance Organizational culture is one of the most influential factors in developing countries in company, So many researchers believe that an important issue to the success of Japan's industry is the attention to the Insurance Organizational culture. One of the main purposes of any kind of Insurance Organization is improving its productivity and since human has a pivotal role in the development of productivity, his demands has key effects on the Insurance Organizational performance. Productivity is defined as maximizing the use of resources, manpower and scientific measures to reduce costs and satisfying employee, managers and consumers. Efforts to improve the efficient use of resources such as human resources, capital, materials, energy and information, the aim of all economic Insurance Organizations and managers of manufacturing firms and service firms. when a there was a strong and cohesive culture, staff gain more knowledge about the Insurance Organization's goals according to the values and norms, sense of responsibility, commitment and create job satisfaction, and whole management was strong, it lead to increase motivation and productivity of employees And ultimately enhance Insurance Organizational performance. The main issues of this study are that does Insurance Organizational culture effects on human resources productivity in SAMAN insurance company? Therefore, we intend to assess the relationship between Insurance Organizational culture elements by the factors affecting the Insurance Organizational efficiency that are Ability, Clarity, Help, Incentive, Evaluation, Validity and Environment.

The main idea of culture comes from sharing in learning processes that have been based upon systematic allocation of resources. The cognitive systems of human that helps in improving thinking and decision making were based upon Insurance Organization culture. The multifaceted set of beliefs, assumptions and values helps in presenting different level of culture by conducting business at an effective manner. The normative glue based upon Insurance Organization culture helps in holding overall management effectiveness. The concept of effective Insurance Organization culture helps in improving business decisions. The survival of culture in an Insurance Organization lies upon national and foreign culture differentiation in culture management. The culture of Insurance Organization has been affected by attitudes, norms and beliefs that lead to strong communication between employees.

1-3-Importance and Necessity of Research

Insurance Organizational culture adapts overtime to cope with the dynamic changes and meet the varying demands of the Insurance Organization in its quest for gaining competitive advantage in all its activities. Therefore, a supportive culture as noted by Ritchie, (2000) is considered as a motivational instrument, which promotes the Insurance Organization to perform smoothly and ensure success in all its endeavours. Thus, the aim of this research is to examine the impact of Insurance Organizational culture on the human resource productivity of SAMAN insurance company as our study case.

The concept of Productivity is used mostly on economic issues and manufacturing because of desperately need of economic restructuring and efficient use of production factors. this severity of attention to this issues gives this mentality that efficiency is summarized only in economic issues while the man as an individual need the productivity culture more than Society economy. This mean that introduction of human resources productivity and economic production is the Cultural productivity of individuals and production factors, because these are the society people that make the community and the favorable society is combine of aware and good management of that community. On the other hand if members of the Insurance Organization do not know the Insurance Organizational culture, they cannot gain consciousness of the nature and goals of the Insurance Organization and thus do not learn how to behave and act well in the system. A strong and consistent Insurance Organizational culture provides hidden patterns for behavior of employees in the Insurance Organizations, subsequently; members gain awareness and commitment about mission and goals of the Insurance Organization. Understanding the Insurance Organizational culture and knowing about its shortcoming and problems by understanding this issues that each Insurance Organization has its own culture, Is inevitable and trying to overcome these shortcomings and enhance the various aspects of personality and human development and health promotion office in the Insurance Organization is necessary. However, given the importance of the impact of Insurance Organizational culture on Insurance Organizational productivity and employee efficiency, we examined this issue that is there any relationship between Insurance Organizational culture and productivity of human resources? And that if there was, witch component of Insurance Organizational culture have the greatest impact on human resources productivity?

1-4-Research Objectives

Objectives

The main objective

Surveying the effect of Specificities of an Insurance Organization's Culture on Human Resource Productivity

Surveying the effect of Human Resource Productivity on Specificities of an Insurance Organization's Culture

Secondary objectives

- Surveying the effect of Specificities of an Insurance Organization's Culture on employee ability
- Surveying the effect of Specificities of an Insurance Organization's Culture on job clarity by staff.
- Surveying the effect of Specificities of an Insurance Organization's Culture on Insurance Organizational help.
- Surveying the effect of Specificities of an Insurance Organization's Culture on employee incentive.
- Surveying the effect of Specificities of an Insurance Organization's Culture on employee evaluation.
- Surveying the effect of Specificities of an Insurance Organization's Culture on employee validity.
- Surveying the effect of Specificities of an Insurance Organization's Culture on employees environmentally.
- Surveying the effect of Human Resource Productivity on Reward systems
- Surveying the effect of Human Resource Productivity on Individual creativity
- Surveying the effect of Human Resource Productivity on Control
- Surveying the effect of Human Resource Productivity on Support
- Surveying the effect of Human Resource Productivity on Clarity
- Surveying the effect of Human Resource Productivity on Risk taking
- Surveying the effect of Human Resource Productivity on Corporate identification
- Surveying the effect of Human Resource Productivity on Conflict taking

1-5-Hypotheses

Main hypothesis:

Specificities of an Insurance Organization's Culture has effect on Human Resource Productivity

Human Resource Productivity has effect on Specificities of an Insurance Organization's Culture

Sub hypothesis:

- Specificities of an Insurance Organization's Culture has impact on employee ability
- Specificities of an Insurance Organization's Culture has effect on job clarity by staff.
- Specificities of an Insurance Organization's Culture has effect on Insurance Organizational help.
- Specificities of an Insurance Organization's Culture has effect on employee incentive.
- Specificities of an Insurance Organization's Culture has effect on employee evaluation.
- Specificities of an Insurance Organization's Culture has effect on employee validity.
- Specificities of an Insurance Organization's Culture has effect on employees environmentally.
- Human Resource Productivity has impact on Reward systems
- Human Resource Productivity has impact on Individual creativity
- Human Resource Productivity has impact on Control
- Human Resource Productivity has impact on Support
- Human Resource Productivity has impact on Clarity
- Human Resource Productivity has impact on Risk taking
- Human Resource Productivity has impact on Corporate identification
- Human Resource Productivity has impact on Conflict taking

1-6-Research Questions

The Main Question

How the Specificities of an Insurance Organization's Culture can impact Human Resource Productivity?

Sub hypothesis:

- Are Specificities of an Insurance Organization's Culture has impact on employee ability?
- Are Specificities of an Insurance Organization's Culture has effect on job clarity by staff?
- Are Specificities of an Insurance Organization's Culture has effect on Insurance Organizational help?
- Are Specificities of an Insurance Organization's Culture has effect on employee incentive?
- Are Specificities of an Insurance Organization's Culture has effect on employee evaluation?
- Are Specificities of an Insurance Organization's Culture has effect on employee validity?
- Are Specificities of an Insurance Organization's Culture has effect on employees environmentally?
- Are Human Resource Productivity has impact on Reward systems?
- Are Human Resource Productivity has impact on Individual creativity?
- Are Human Resource Productivity has impact on Control?
- Are Human Resource Productivity has impact on Support?
- Are Human Resource Productivity has impact on Clarity?
- Are Human Resource Productivity has impact on Risk taking?
- Are Human Resource Productivity has impact on corporate identification?
- Are Human Resource Productivity has impact on Conflict taking?

1-7-Time of research execution

The time of implementation of this research is in the first half of 2019.

Research Area

The domain of this research is SAMAN Insurance Company.

1-8-Definition of Concepts and Terminology

Definition of Insurance Organizational Culture

Although over 150 definitions of culture have been identified (Kroeber & Kluckhohn, 1952), the two main disciplinary foundations of Insurance Organizational culture are sociological (e.g., Insurance Organizations have cultures) and anthropological (e.g., Insurance Organizations are cultures). Within each of these disciplines, two different approaches to culture were developed: a functional approach (e.g., culture emerges from collective behavior) and a semiotic approach (e.g., culture resides in individual interpretations and cognitions). The primary distinctions are differences between culture as an attribute possessed by Insurance Organizations versus culture as a metaphor for describing what Insurance Organizations are. The former approach assumes that researchers and managers can identify differences among Insurance Organizational cultures, can change cultures, and can empirically measure cultures. The latter perspective assumes that nothing exists in Insurance Organizations except culture, and one encounters culture anytime one rubs up against any Insurance Organizational phenomena. Culture is a potential predictor of other Insurance Organizational outcomes (e.g., effectiveness) in the former perspective, whereas in the latter perspective it is a concept to be explained independent of any other phenomenon.

A review of the literature on culture in Insurance Organizational studies reveals that a majority of writers have come to an agreement that culture refers to the taken-for-granted values, underlying assumptions, expectations, and definitions present which characterize Insurance Organizations and their members (that is, they have adopted the functional, sociological perspective). Most discussions of Insurance Organizational culture (Cameron & Ettington, 1988; O'Reilly & Chatman, 1996; Schein, 1996) agree with the idea that culture is a socially constructed attribute of Insurance Organizations which serves as the "social glue" binding an Insurance Organization together. Culture represents "how things are around here," or the prevailing ideology that people carry inside their heads, thus, culture affects the way Insurance Organization members think, feel, and behave.

Importantly, the concept of Insurance Organizational *culture* is distinct from the concept of Insurance Organizational *climate.* Climate refers to temporary attitudes, feelings, and perceptions of individuals (Schneider, 1990). Culture is an enduring, slow to change, core characteristic of Insurance Organizations; climate, because it is based on attitudes, can change quickly and dramatically. Culture refers to implicit, often indiscernible aspects of Insurance Organizations; climate refers to more overt, observable attributes of Insurance Organizations. Culture includes core values and consensual interpretations about how things are; climate includes individualistic perspectives that are modified frequently as situations change and new information is encountered. The approach to change in this article focuses on cultural attributes rather than climate attributes. It considers the "links among cognitions, human interactions, and tangible symbols or artifacts typifying an Insurance Organization" (Detert, Schroeder, & Mauriel, 2000:853), or, in other words, "the way things are" in the Insurance Organization rather than people's transitory attitudes about them.

Unfortunately, most people are unaware of their culture until it is challenged, until they experience a new culture, or until culture is made overt and explicit through, for example, a framework or model. Most people did not wake up this morning, for example, making a conscious decision about which language to speak. It is only when confronted with a different language, or asked specific questions about language, that people become aware that language is one of their defining attributes. Similarly, culture is undetectable most of the time because it is not challenged or consciously articulated. Measuring culture, therefore, has presented a challenge to Insurance Organizational scholars and change agents.

Human resource management

'Human resources' is the term used today to describe the key ingredient of any health system: the people running it - from the cleaner and the gardener, to the heart surgeon, the volunteer and the top administrator.

In the past other terms were used: 'health manpower', with its problematic gender connotation, 'health workforce', etc. Today, the term 'human resources' seem to have become widely accepted and that is why we will be using it throughout this module.

The term flags the fact that the people running the health system are indeed a resource that has to be developed and nurtured. In fact, they are the most crucial and the most expensive resource in the health system. Conventionally, between 65% and 80% of the entire health budget is spent on human resources, leaving a relatively small proportion for everything else: drugs, buildings, equipment, transport and other running costs.

Furthermore, human resources require the longest preparatory time of all health resources and cannot be improvised. The training of health human resources is subject to the rigidities of the health and education systems and yet, personnel, unlike other health resources, cannot be stored or discarded. They have to be available in the right numbers and type at the right time – no more and no less than is needed. This is the most important challenge of human resource planning and production, i.e. the education and training of health professionals.

Lastly, because their skills are subject to obsolescence, particularly in our times of rapidly developing technology and knowledge, human resource abilities and skills need to be updated and improved through continuous development, training and supervision – a major challenge for human resource production and management.

Strangely, what is often forgotten or neglected in health planning is the fact that this most crucial and most expensive of health resources consists of human beings, people with hopes, aspirations and feelings, and who live within families and communities. We will see in this unit that the neglect of the human aspect of human resource development has severe consequences for the system as a whole, and has contributed to the negative track record of Human Resource Development (HRD) within health sector transformation in the past decades.

Human Resource Development (or HRD for short) encompasses the planning for, development and management of human resources. Within the health system, these three components may each be controlled by a different authority, which makes co-ordination between their functions difficult. As a consequence formal mechanisms, such a Human Resource Planning or Development Unit may be necessary.

1-9-Methods for collecting information (field, library, etc.):

In this research, library studies have been used to investigate theoretical literature, problem histories, research topics, research structures, etc. For this purpose, books, articles, documents, and internal and external dissertations are used to get more familiar with the subject of research and after necessary scans, they are used as needed. Information can be gathered in a variety of ways, in different places and from a variety of sources. Data gathering methods consist of face-to-face interviews, telephone interviews, computer interviews; face-to-face interviews, email and e-mail questionnaires; viewing of people or events by recording (or without recording) audio and video and various motivational techniques such as screening tests.

1-10-Research methods

Since this research has been done on HRM, Insurance Organizational culture and its results can be applied in practice, it is an applied research and is also a descriptive-survey based on the research project and is of a nature, analytical and Exploration is done using a combination of quantitative and qualitative models. In this research, data was collected using deep interview method and questionnaire and information and tables were completed by a survey of experts, experts and decision makers of Insurance companies (SAMAN Insurance Company).

1-11-Statistical Society:

If a satisfactory result is to be obtained from the sample, it should be fully aware of the set of activities and steps used to select the sample. The first step in this field is to determine the research objectives. In order to clarify this goal, we first need to define the statistical society we intend to select from the study sample. (Delavar, 2008: 102) SAMAN Insurance company has been considered as a statistical society in this research, with a number of customers selected by 300 people. A simple random sampling method was used for sampling. In a simple random sampling method, each element of the community to be selected has the same odds. Choosing a sample is important, and the larger the sample, the closer it is to the characteristics of the community, and the more general its results are more rational. A good example is a cost-effective example, as well as a representative of the entire community. The statistical sample in this research is part of the statistical society. Simple random sampling method.

1-12-Information Analysis Methodology:

The present study will be used by combining quantitative and qualitative methods with a mixed or mixed approach. Combined research methods are a research project with philosophical assumptions as well as exploration methods. The basic assumption in composite research is that combining qualitative and quantitative approaches to each of the approaches alone will provide a better understanding of the research problem. Combined research involves collecting and analyzing quantitative and qualitative data. Quantitative data are obtained through a closed response tool such as a questionnaire. In contrast to qualitative data, reciprocal information is formed, for example, through interviews.

Researchers in combined research consider the exploration project to be more prominent and they argue that in the exploratory blending scheme, the researcher is seeking to identify the uncertain position and examine the process (including a sequence of activities) will pay. To do this, we first collect qualitative data and then collect quantitative data. In this type of project, the quality data is given more importance; therefore, the researcher first qualitatively examines the subject of the research with limited participants and then proceeds on the basis of qualitative findings relative to the construction of the tool.

With regard to the above, and since in this research, according to the main objective, which is to investigate the Specificities of an Insurance Organization's Culture has effect on Human Resource Productivity, in order to in-depth study and further understanding of the topic of the exploratory design, which is a hybrid method Is used. In the qualitative stage, in order to identify the main variables, the classification system or classification system has been developed, or a new theory has been developed, and in the secondary stage, these results are more accurately evaluated or studied. The researcher intends to identify new categories according to the qualitative data, and then, in the quantitative stage, examine these categories in different samples.

The purpose of the second stage is to test or review these findings more accurately. In addition, the researcher may achieve identification of emerging classifications from qualitative data. Therefore, the main purpose of collecting qualitative data is to explore the concepts, categories and their relationship with the respondent's reaction to the phenomenon. Qualitative findings have shaped and influenced a small part.

Qualitative Division Analysis Method

SPSS software is used to analyze the data. In this software, data are analyzed in two sections: descriptive statistics and inferential statistics. Descriptive statistics section includes frequency, mean, standard deviation and statistical tables and charts. In the inferential statistics section, Kolmogorov-Smirnov test was first used to determine the normal or abnormal data. If the data are normal, Pearson correlation coefficient will be used to test the hypotheses and the regression coefficient will be used to measure the extent and severity of the effects.

1-13-Research Structure

The present study is presented in five chapters. The first chapter describes the generalities of the research. The second chapter is devoted to the study of theoretical principles and internal and external research to support the hypotheses and research methodology. The third chapter deals with the methodology of the research and describes the statistical society, sampling method, data collection method and its analysis method. In Chapter 4, the data collected is analyzed through a field study, and in Chapter 5, the research findings are presented and based on which research and applied research suggestions are presented. Figure 1-1 shows the structure of the research.

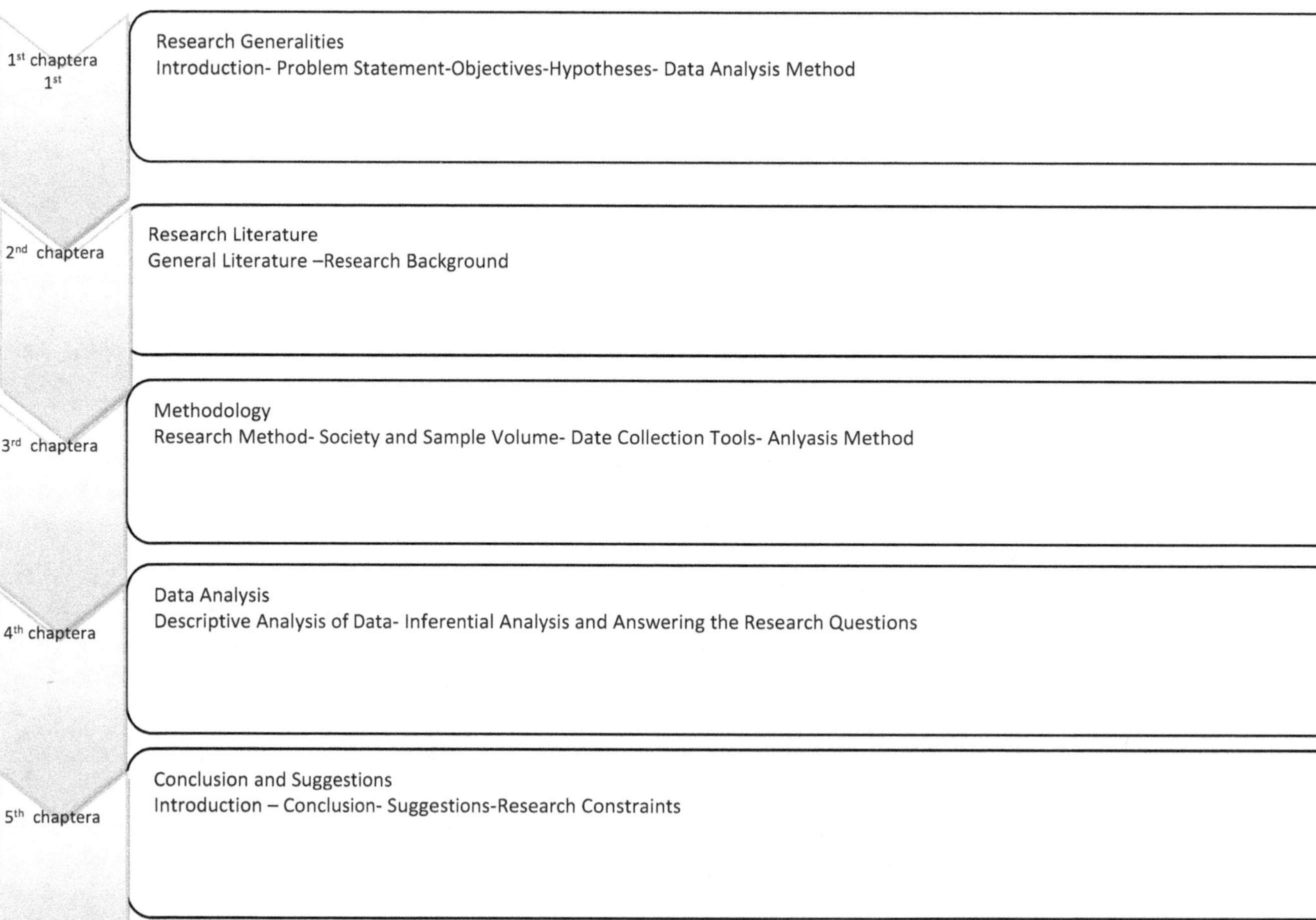

Figure 1-1. Research structure

1-14-Chapter Summaries

This chapter focuses on the overall research, including the subject matter of the research, the reasons for choosing a subject, the importance and necessity of it, the statement of the subject, the objectives of the research, the research questions, the research hypotheses, the variables of the research, the research community, the method of data collection and operational definitions of the terms and variables of the research was studied.

Chapter II

Research Background and Theoretical Foundations

2-1-Introduction

Insurance Organizational culture is conceptualized as shared beliefs and values within the Insurance Organization that helps to shape the behavior patterns of employees (Kotter and Heskett, 1992). Gordon and Cummins (1989) define Insurance Organization culture as the drive that recognizes the efforts and contributions of the Insurance Organizational members and provides holistic understanding of what and how to be achieve , how goals are interrelated, and how each employee could attain goals. Hofstede (1990) summarizes Insurance Organization culture as collective process of the mind that differentiates the members of one group from the other one. Thus, we can deduce from above definitions that Insurance Organizational culture could be the means of keeping employees in line and acclimatizing them towards Insurance Organizational objectives. Deal and Kennedy, (1982) recognizes the link between culture and Insurance Organizational excellent performances via its human resource development programmes. These cultural values and human resource development programmes are consistent with Insurance Organizational chosen strategies that led to successful Insurance Organizations. The Insurance Organizational culture is outlined in Schein (1990) as overall phenomenon of the Insurance Organization such as natural settings, the rite and rituals, climate, values and programmes of the company e.g. performance management, training and development, recruitment and selection, etc. According to Martins and Terblanche (2003), culture is deeply associated with values and beliefs shared by personnel in an Insurance Organization. Insurance Organizational culture relates the employees to Insurance Organization's values, norms, stories, beliefs and principles and incorporates these assumptions into them as activity and behavioural set of standards. Klein, (1996) positioned Insurance Organizational culture as the core of Insurance Organization's activities which has aggregate impact on its overall effectiveness and the quality of its product and services. Schein (2004) defined Insurance Organizational culture as a dynamic force within the Insurance Organization which is revolving, engaging and interactive and it is shaped up by the employees and management gestures, behaviours and attitudes.

2.2 Theoretical Foundations of Research

Insurance Organizational Culture

Insurance Organizational culture has proven to be very elusive because of the lack of a single definition that is generally accepted by all Insurance Organizational culture literatures. One of the issues involving culture is that it is defined both in terms of its causes and effects (Shili, 2008). Insurance Organizational culture is a complex network of values and norms that guides an individual's behaviors. It involves a set of beliefs, values, assumptions and experience that are acquired through learning, socializing and sharing by members of social unit such as people in the Insurance Organization (Rousseau, 1990) Almost all the definitions of culture emphasizes the Insurance Organizational assumptions developed, nurtured and mentored consciously or unconsciously over Insurance Organization's life cycle;, these includes experiences, norms, values, philosophy and rituals that hold the Insurance Organization together; its portrait, self-image, inner workings, interaction with the outside environment where some of the values are kept in written form while others are unwritten but yet adhered to strictly (Schein, 1984). The culture of an Insurance Organization is sometimes dynamic in nature, particularly after doing effective strength and weakness analysis, out of which can be eliminated and advantages retained and strengthened (Shumen, 2009). A valid Insurance Organizational culture is called corporate culture (Shumen, 2009). Schein (1984) argues that we can describe "how" a group constructs its environment and which behavior patterns are discernible among the way it does its things. It is clear that Insurance Organizational culture is a process that the Insurance Organizational founders, top management and employees learn, socialize and adopt over time (Schein, 1984). It selects the best culture that suits the Insurance Organization's objectives and that can be easily be accepted by wider environment (Robbins & Judge, 2009). Insurance Organizational culture is the normative glue that holds an Insurance Organization together (Tichy, Fombrun & Devanna, 1982). Support by Schein (1990), in a more comprehensive fashion, argued that culture, as values and behaviors that are believed to lead to success and are thus taught to new members. Forehand and Gilmer (1964) suggest that culture is the set of characteristics that describe an Insurance Organization and distinguish it from others. Alvesson and Berg (1992) state that, Insurance Organizational culture is a management tool that helps in work rationalization and efficiency thinking: an attempt to develop control mechanisms that are not based on compulsion or on direction. Parker (2000) argues that workers strive to get to command themselves or each other. The manager's task is considered to be the creation of a culture and its manipulation. The power of cultural theories is seen particularly in fields in which direct control and guidance mechanisms are difficult or impossible to maintain (Parker, 2000). Collins (1998) sums up the matter by stating that cultures are historically developed, socially maintained and individually interpreted. Every culture, however, has an in-built propensity to merge behavior, which happens by creating common norms and a shared social identity; such absolute behavior within a given Insurance Organization is called corporate culture (Collins, 1998).

ELEMENTS OF ORGANISATIONAL CULTURE

To understand organisational culture it is very important to know all its elements. Authors are not unanimous about what are the elements of the organisational culture. According to Armstrong (Žugaj, Cingula, 1992; 209) there are three important elements of organisational culture. These are: 1) organisation value, 2) organisation climate and 3) manager style.

(1) Organisation values represent everything what is considered to be valuable for the organisation and what would have to and ought to happen. They are expressed as purpose, mission or strategic objectives of the organisation.

(2) Organisation climate is the company culture characterised by experience and understanding of the employees and/or by quality of organisation value. This climate has impact on motivation, productivity, creativity and innovations.

(3) Manager style represents behaviour of managers and the management of the organisation when conducting their affairs. Literature abounds in descriptions of numerous management styles, which in most cases include either narrower or broader scope within two extreme styles: autocratic and democratic.

Megginson, Mosley and Pietri Jr. (1989; 377) believe that the organisational culture consist of the following elements: ceremonies, rituals, heroes, narrators, preachers, informers, gossipers, spies, myths and legends.

Ceremonies are a part of organisational culture which are usually planned in advance to express various aspects of cultural impact and contribution to creation of a specific stimulating climate and motivation in the organisation. Success of an individual contributes to the organisation itself and requires recognition. Recognition receiving ceremony significantly points out motivation effects. The way the ceremony is organised is deeply impacted by organisational culture.

Rituals, as an element of organisational culture, are detailed procedures and methods. They are performed consistently, on a periodical or regular basis. They include a very broad scope of activities: work, play, recognition or manager meeting. Rituals represent the way of conducting a specific ceremony.

Heroes are persons whose success brings the mythical and the human together. Their existence is essential for the organisational culture, because improvement of certain standards can be achieved only by them, but still with presence of a much needed boost.

From the viewpoint of organisational culture **narrators** may have a very positive but also a negative role. Their narrations may have effects on creation of sound company culture.

In distinction from narrators, who more or less spontaneously and systematically deal with an event within the organisation, **preachers** calculatedly express their premeditated views on events in the organisation. Their role is to understand fully the views of the organisation and to accept them as their own for a longer time period.

Informers are persons who inform of the fulfilled level of certain assignments performed by some employees in the organisation. In this way it is possible to exercise control over the employees' work..

Gossipers are persons which spread superficial, unverified and slanderous information about persons and events in the organisation. They can be very detrimental to the internal homogenisation of the organisation.

Spies are person who may work in or against the interest of the organisation. Some spies have dual and/or multiple role. They are useful for the organisation if they collect for it important economy-related and other information.

Myths and legends are significant elements of the organisational culture. They express social awareness through stories about the past and present events in the organisation, about its heroes and achieved success. They provide the basis for creation of legends, i.e. stories with real base which lost their objective accuracy by narrating (Zvonarević, 1985; 310-311).

In addition to the indicated classification of elements of organisational culture, there is also a classification according to: values, standards, attitudes and beliefs, habits and rituals, language and communications, and symbols (Bahtijarević-Šiber et al., red. Kapustić, 1991; 204).

Values represent strategy operationalization, and are related to the priorities which are significant for existence and development of the organisation.

Standards may or may not be written, they are related to the procedure by which something should be achieved. They show what kind of behaviour is expected and appreciated, and what kind of behaviour requires punishment in the organisation.

The most elusive part of the organisation culture are **attitudes and beliefs**. This element represents basic ideals and principles of organisation behaviour.

For **customs and rituals**, as elements of organisational culture, one might say that these are operational and established forms of behaviour. They are used to stimulate and intensify the identification of employees with their organisation, and to create the way of behaviour and interrelations.

A specific form of organisational culture are **language and communication**. Language is a sign of a certain social status of employees in an organisation. It is a close friend and reflects everything what is going on in the organisation. Language is used to persuade, to order and express emotional relief. A person or an organisation expresses its identity by communication. By its verbal or non-verbal communication, an organisation or an individual may show its or his/her level of culture.

Symbols, as a constituent part of any organisational culture, convey basic ideas about priority values of the organisation. They represent external visual signs of the organisation. The floor where a manager office is located, the way the office is decorated, is his/her office furnished with paintings or not, which car does he/she drive, the sign on the door, the place where he/she has launch, tea or coffee, place where he/she parks a car, etc., represent very important status symbols, symbols of social differentiation, and of culture as a whole. Changes in organisational culture, as recorded recently, show tendency towards removal of such external symbols and towards equality, following the example of Japanese firms (Bahtijarević-Šiber, et. al., red, Kapustić, 1991; 204).

The indicated classification of elements of organisational culture suggest that there are two levels of organisational culture: the visible and the invisible one. The visible signs of culture are: ceremonies, slogans, symbols, stories, the way of dressing, behaviour, and alike. The invisible signs of the organisational culture are: common values, hypotheses, beliefs, attitudes and emotions (Sikavica, Novak, 1993; 367).

Knowledge of the elements of organisational culture provides the basis for forming and use of the organisational culture to achieve the objectives of the organisation. In this case, the concept of entrepreneurship which is used to give an impetus to development of small and medium-sized companies, could not have free use of one important creativity development instrument. In fact, there are some young companies which may have a well-developed business philosophy, attitudes towards creativity and other important elements of organisation culture, although these elements have never been formalised (Žugaj, Cingula, 1992; 210).

HOW IS CULTURE CREATED?

Modern cultures do not spring forth out of nothing. Cultures build on existing cultures. A new business may create its own unique corporate culture, but that business is not starting with a blank slate; rather, it is inheriting its initial culture from the dominant culture in which it is located and the cultural values brought by the founders and early employees. It is thus possible for a culture to inherit from multiple parent cultures.

Forming Subcultures

Cultures also differentiate, or form subcultures, based on specific situational needs. Ed Schein observes that all businesses form three distinct subcultures: executives, engineers, and operators. The executive subculture is concerned with making; the Insurance Organization run, the engineers with solving the problems faced by the Insurance Organization, and the operators with actually implementing the solutions and dealing with the outside world. Executives create rules and mechanisms to make the Insurance Organization function smoothly—we call it bureaucracy. Engineers seek to develop elegant solutions that cannot be screwed up by people. (As evidence, despite all the complaints and problems with batteries in Apple's iPods, the iPhone still does not have a user-replaceable battery. To design a product with one would violate a cultural belief about making the device elegant and hard to damage. As a further example along those lines, Apple now sells a new laptop that does not have a user-replaceable battery.)

On a larger scale, subcultures form in response to Insurance Organizational needs, geographical constraints, and anything else that requires adapting to various environmental conditions. A large corporation, such as IBM, has subcultures broken out by country and task. Countercultures also form within the larger culture. A counterculture in this context is a subculture that deliberately rejects certain aspects of the parent culture while still remaining committed to the parent culture's goals. For example, during IBM's blue suit and tie heyday, the research division was determinedly informal. Unlike the rest of IBM, jeans and T-shirts were common, and ties were rare.

How Leaders Shape Culture

Within an Insurance Organization, leaders have tremendous power to shape the culture through a variety of means. At the most basic level, the example a leader sets will form the basis for much of the culture. The culture of the once mighty Digital Equipment Corporation (DEC) reflected the beliefs and attitudes of its founder, Ken Olsen. DEC was once the darling of the computer industry, an incredibly successful company during the 1960s, '70s, and into the '80s. It was, in many ways, the Microsoft of its day, the company that many believed would destroy IBM. Today it no longer exists. Olsen, an MIT-educated engineer, believed that all ideas should be tested through argument and debate; if the idea couldn't be proved wrong, the developers had the right to go ahead with the idea and let the market decide. This approach served DEC very well in its early days. However, because Olsen never really believed in the PC, the culture at DEC was to not take the PC seriously. As a result, and because no one group could convince the other groups they were wrong, DEC ended up producing three different, incompatible versions of the PC. The net result was that the market decided not to support any of DEC's PCs. What a leader pays attention to and how a leader respond to a crisis, deals with disagreement, treats those around him, and behaves in general will all feed into the culture of the Insurance Organization.

If, as I've often seen, a leader treats every unexpected problem or unanticipated roadblock as a major crisis, so will the employees. If a leader takes the view that every problem could have been avoided and therefore when something goes wrong, heads must roll, the resulting culture will usually be one of blame and finger-pointing. If a leader views mistakes as a natural part of learning, exploring, and experimenting, the resulting culture is likely going to be one that supports innovation.

Beyond actions, leaders shape the culture through the stories that they tell and the stories that are told about them. The stories a leader tells help to inform employees about what the leader considers important. At one start-up I worked for many years ago, the CEO used to talk disparagingly about his interactions with the customers. Every customer was an idiot, an incompetent, or both. It wasn't long before this attitude permeated the company. The effects could be seen in every area, from the engineers writing the software, to tech support, to marketing, and so on. Sloppy design decisions were made because, after all, the customers were "too stupid" to know the difference.

Even when the founder, or other influential leader, is no longer around, his or her legacy lives on, reinforcing the values of the culture. When I worked for IBM many years ago, there were countless stories about Tom Watson: how when an IBM employee was badly injured and his family killed in a car accident, Watson was there at the hospital when the man woke up, promising to cover the medical bills and do whatever he could; how, when a train derailment injured a large number of IBMers on their way to the World's Fair, Watson drove out in the middle of the night to organize the rescue effort; and other such anecdotes. These stories underscored the cultural meme that IBM took care of its employees no matter what. Stories like these, whether told at one of the largest companies in the world or at a small nonprofit, serve to reinforce and transmit the Insurance Organization's culture.

HOW IS CULTURE TRANSMITTED?

Culture is transmitted in a variety of ways. For our gorillas, the transmission is through being beaten up by other gorillas if you happen to go after those bananas. More generally, though, cultures are transmitted through formal and informal means. Formal methods include education, religion, and family values. Informal methods include stories, songs, artifacts, and social signals.

Education is a fundamental tool of cultural transmission, be it societal or Insurance Organizational culture. What American students are taught in school shapes their understanding of American culture; what employees are taught on the job shapes their understanding of their corporate culture. Sometimes, these may be in contradiction to aspects of the larger culture.

The artifacts of our culture include stories, songs, institutions, symbols, and buildings. Artifacts can also include how we use time, where we park, how we address others, where people live, and any other choice that might be made within the domain of the culture. The artifacts are constant reminders of how culture works and what it stands for. The meanings of those artifacts, however, may change or may be viewed differently by different groups within the culture. One of the most difficult tasks for a newcomer to a culture is to determine what meanings the artifacts have; it doesn't matter whether the culture in question is a foreign country or a new corporation. For example, having a parking spot near the doors might be a sign of high status in one company, meaningless in another and low status in a third. Offices on higher floors of a building sometimes indicate higher status.

WHAT ARE THE ADVANTAGES AND DISADVANTAGES OF CULTURE?

To digress briefly, the concept of automaticity is extremely familiar to athletes and teachers. A skill is said to be automatized when one can perform that skill with little or no conscious effort. Think of a basketball player dribbling a ball, or a student reciting a poem from memory. In each case, the actions are so ingrained that they are executed automatically when the appropriate stimulus is presented. Relatively complex series of actions can be practiced and automatized, a process sometimes referred to as "chunking." The advantage is that the chunk can be performed without calling upon cognitive resources. The disadvantage is that an automatized chunk is very hard to change; it's even difficult to interrupt yourself once the chunk is triggered. If you are interrupted, it's often extremely disorienting and virtually impossible to pick up where you left off. Instead, you usually have to start again at the beginning. Cultures operate in an analogous fashion: sequences of behavior come to be taken for granted, and once started, cannot easily be stopped. The advantage of this is that resources are not constantly expended reanalyzing the same situation. The disadvantage is that the situation may be more nuanced than the chunked behavior can handle.

Cultures also provide members with common ground in a set of shared and agreed-upon values and beliefs. The stronger and more prevalent these values are, the easier it is for members of the culture to work together and form strong bonds among one another. Culture thus acts as a unifying force among people who are steeped in the culture but can be a repulsive force for those who are not. Thus, new members to the Insurance Organization, that is, new members of the culture, need to be educated as to the cultural values and how those values are manifest.

What makes understanding culture particularly difficult is that two cultures can develop completely different ways of manifesting the same stated values. For instance, both the PC and the Mac claim to be easy to use. They both are, but in very different ways, and for very different audiences. PC hardware and software can be easily customized by the user, provided that user is reasonably knowledgeable about the technology. The PC user can do almost anything but can also screw up the system quite thoroughly. The Mac, on the other hand, provides a very slick, clean interface that may limit what you can do but also prevents major disasters. Similar cultural values, very different results.

Ultimately, a culture can be thought of as an encapsulation of concepts, values, and behaviors. Members of a culture will default to the culturally determined heuristics if they haven't developed a more specific version or override of their own. The reasons behind the values and behaviors are hidden within the encapsulation and become "it's just how we do things."

WHAT MAKES A SUCCESSFUL CULTURE?

A culture is successful if it is in harmony with its environment and unsuccessful if it is unable to function in its environment. The environment is the world in which the culture operates. Here's the catch: environments change faster than cultures. When the environment changes, the mechanisms of the culture may no longer be valid. As we've already discussed, a culture is an encapsulation of information and procedures for dealing with the world. The advent of the PC changed the business environment for IBM, and the company found it difficult indeed to adjust. The bursting of the tech bubble in 2000 turned Sun Microsystems from one of the world's top companies to one that could not function in the brave new post-bubble world. Today, with the accelerating shift from desktop computers to mobile devices and the Internet, Microsoft is still, in many ways, playing catch-up. Just because those procedures are no longer working doesn't mean that they immediately fall out of favor. First, the procedures are chunked, so they are carried out at an almost reflexive level. Second, the prospect of change can, and often does, engender more fear and anxiety than the actual failure of the outmoded procedures. Acknowledging that these fundamental cultural lessons are wrong is tantamount to admitting that the world does not work the way we thought it did. Some cultures can adjust; others cannot. A third, and potentially more serious, issue is that the world, and human behavior, is not digital: it is not either 1 or 0. In other words, rarely does a behavior go from working 100 percent of the time to not working 100 percent of the time.

Rapid environmental change is not instantaneous. Rather, the change occurs over a period of time. A behavior that worked most of the time in the old environment starts failing more and more frequently. Initially, this is hard to distinguish from the normal, occasional failures. The initial reaction is to "try harder" while doing the same thing. So long as the behavior still works sometimes, periodically these increased efforts, these "sales drives" or what have you, will appear to be making a difference. This is a phenomenon known as intermittent reinforcement, and, in this context, it creates an illusion of success. A set of behaviors that are reinforced intermittently can become even more ingrained than they were before the intermittent reinforcement began!

Thus, as the environment moves away from the culture, the culture's reflexive efforts to apply the lessons of success can actually lock the culture into increasingly nonfunctional behaviors! In general, the best way to change a culture as the environment changes is not to introduce something new but to strengthen an existing aspect of the culture.

In 1992, IBM imploded. The company posted a loss for the first time in its history, closed down numerous divisions, and even instituted layoffs. IBM's survival was in serious question. However, IBM's culture contained a very strong ethic of "analyze the problem, determine the solution, and execute the solution even if it's unpleasant." IBM realized that it needed a fresh perspective, so it brought in Lou Gerstner, the first non-IBMer to become CEO. As Ed Schein points out, Gerstner came from a very similar marketing background to IBM's founder; Tom Watson, Sr. Gerstner didn't so much change IBM's culture as revitalize an aspect of it that had become dormant. Over the years, IBM's engineering culture had become dominant, and the marketing culture had faded into the background. In restoring the latter, Gerstner also restored the company's fortunes.

WHERE IS CULTURE?

Culture is in the minds of the people who comprise the culture. When a culture is threatened by something in its environment, be that a new idea or another culture, it becomes more itself. In other words, those cultural elements that appear to be most appropriate to reducing the anxiety are triggered to deal with the threat. More diverse cultures are likely to attempt multiple simultaneous solutions, while more monolithic cultures are more likely to view all problems as nails for which they are the hammers.

For example, let's look at a company called "Shrinks-R-Us," or SRU for short. (The company and example are real, but the name and various descriptive details have been changed to preserve anonymity.) SRU provides mental health services and is paid primarily through insurance. Over the years, SRU developed a system of paperwork that is the envy of bureaucrats everywhere. Why? No one seems to know, and it no longer matters. What matters is that today paperwork is seen as the answer to every problem. If employees make too many mistakes or attempt to streamline the process, the company adds another layer of paperwork. One therapist commented that the paperwork is so complex they have to use checklists—meta-paperwork—to make sure that they've done it all. There is even a quality-assurance committee that reviews the internal paperwork with a fine-toothed comb, sends back anything with an error, and puts out weekly reports that people are expected to read. The bulk of therapists' time is controlled by the need to do the paperwork. Quality is no longer about the success of therapy, but the accuracy of the paperwork. Fundamentally, the culture has developed the Insurance Organizational equivalent of obsessive-compulsive disorder (OCD).

Now, compare SRU to "ShrinkWrap," another company in the same mental health industry and in the same broad geographic area. (Again, the company's name and various identifying details have been changed where necessary to preserve anonymity.) Both SRU and ShrinkWrap host a number of psychology interns at their sites. Both are required to provide supervision and training for the interns, which includes reviewing their notes and treatment plans and monitoring their work with patients.

ShrinkWrap requires that interns keep notes, as does SRU. However, that is about the limit of the paperwork at ShrinkWrap. At SRU, in the words of one intern, "I couldn't sneeze without running it by my supervisor." At Shrink-Wrap, on the other hand, interns sometimes wonder if anyone even knows what they are doing. However, as one intern observed, "Any time something came up, my supervisor was clearly familiar with the case." At SRU, no one is trusted to do anything right; everything must be documented, checked, and rechecked. Mistakes are not tolerated and result in an immediate decrease in autonomy through the imposition of more paperwork. At ShrinkWrap, the assumption appears to be that if you bring in competent people and educate them about what is expected, you can trust them to get it right. The inevitable mistakes will be treated as part of the learning process, and people will be quietly educated as to the correct course of action in the future.

As these examples illustrate, similar companies in similar businesses and similar geographic areas can produce extremely different cultures, but both cultures respond to stress by becoming more themselves. SRU, being more monolithic, has one response to every problem. ShrinkWrap, with its more diverse culture, tends to attempt multiple solutions simultaneously.

HOW CAN CULTURE BE CHANGED?

SRU and ShrinkWrap have developed very different ways of responding to their very similar environments. In both of these Insurance Organizations, it is highly likely that the original beliefs of the founders shaped the culture into what it is today. However, when the founders move on, it is equally likely that nothing will change. Neither Insurance Organization will easily tolerate a new CEO who seeks to change the existing culture too radically or too quickly.

The Cultural Immune Response

One of the problems DEC had in its later years, as did Atari, and Apple under John Sculley, was a CEO who didn't share the culture's fundamental culture. In general, the leader of a cultural entity, be that entity company or country, has tremendous power to influence the entity. However, the degree to which the leader meshes with the existing culture will determine his success. When there is a mismatch, the culture will reject the interloper in much the same way as the immune system will respond to a virus. The ideas of the leader are actively or passively opposed, and the members of the culture may leave, become discouraged, or experience other signs of stress and depression. The leader may be forced out, as happened to John Sculley, or the Insurance Organization may be destroyed, as happened to DEC. There is a great deal of truth to the old belief that the health of the king is the health of the land, or at least of the Insurance Organization.

Remember that culture is a road map of how the world works. The longer that culture has been in place, the more successful the Insurance Organization has been, and the more people like the way things are working and are happy with the current situation, the stronger the culture will be. The stronger the culture, the more the road map is trusted. The more the road map is trusted, the harder it is to change.

When a new leader comes in who clashes with the culture, problems will immediately arise. It doesn't matter whether we're talking about a group leader or a CEO, although, in general, the smaller the group, the weaker the culture—simply because it is not distributed over as many people. What the new leader is effectively doing is saving, "Everything you know, everything you believe in, is wrong. Trust me. Follow me. I have the truth."

Now, I suspect that many of you reading that last paragraph are rolling your eyes and thinking, "Yeah, right. It can't be that big a deal!"

Let's consider the situation. For the members of the culture, this road map—this view of the world—is their common bond. It's the thing that holds the Insurance Organization together. By providing structure and predictability, culture reduces anxiety and promotes a feeling of security. Remember also that culture quickly becomes largely unconscious. Behaviors are chunked, no longer thought about on a conscious level.

Then someone comes along and says, "No, no, that's all wrong." Imagine being in that position. How- would you feel? How did you feel the last time your company announced major changes or restructuring?

When a new leader's approach contradicts the fundamental, underlying values of the culture, employees are caught in a state of cognitive dissonance. Very briefly, cognitive dissonance is a state in which people are forced to hold two or more contradictory ideas in their heads at one time. When at least some of the ideas that they are holding are not even at a conscious level, it makes the situation worse. People will seek to move away from a situation that induces cognitive dissonance. The problem is, they may not move to where you want them to go.

In this case, the new CEO is telling them to do things that they "know" in their hearts are wrong. Moreover, most CEOs will make the situation worse by engaging in logical arguments. This is a situation that is less about logic than emotion, a topic we'll cover in more depth in Chapter 7. When logic fails, as it usually will in a cultural mismatch, the CEO will often resort to threats and punishment. The employees feel increasingly trapped and resentful. Some will reluctantly comply, despite feeling guilty that they are betraying their inner beliefs and exposing themselves to the anxiety of their cultural road map not being correct. Others will try to quietly or openly undermine the CEO. Others might try keeping their heads down and hoping that the situation gets better. Some will go along and may well be seen as traitors by the rest. Some will leave. In short, the Insurance Organization becomes ill.

Strategies for Successful Change

Although it is possible for the CEO or senior management to ram through changes in the culture, this will often have unanticipated consequences. Because cultural values are tightly linked, the more central the value being altered or removed, the more pressure there is to restore the preexisting cultural norm. Remember, cultures are self-reinforcing. Cultural values and beliefs support one another, and when an attempt is made to alter a cultural belief, the existing network of ideas pulls back.

The management team, however, does have the power to simply change a policy. If that policy reflects a cultural value in the company, then the change may be far-reaching and unpredictable. For example, in the mid-1990s, IBM abandoned Tom Watson's long-held policy of full employment for life: you took care of the company and the company took care of you. It was a mutually beneficial, symbiotic relationship. IBM was a rock that employees knew would always be there for them. Then it all changed. In response to changing economic conditions, IBM decided that it could no longer afford to maintain full employment. The end of full employment was the psychological equivalent of an earthquake.

In October 2009, the Wall Street Journal reported that IBM executive Robert Moffat, "a senior vice president and a close confidant of IBM Chief Executive Samuel Palmisano," was arrested for insider trading. While it's impossible to fully identify all the ramifications and permutations in such a complex system, when Robert Moffat was arrested, IBM discussion groups on the Net brought up the point over and over that when full employment was removed, so was the source of a great deal of loyalty to the company. The two values had become intimately tied together. While no one condoned Moffat's behavior, there was also a strong sense of "what did you expect?"

Since my approach to changing the culture is strongly influenced by Ed Schein, I'll be drawing heavily on material from Ed Schein's work, in particular The Corporate Culture Survival Guide.

Let's start by recognizing that cultures are constantly changing and adapting. The process, however, is generally extremely slow and usually undirected. New lessons are learned over time and incorporated into different aspects of the culture. At the same time, old lessons may fall into disuse. They are not so much forgotten as become dormant, waiting for an appropriate trigger to activate them. It can take a very long time for a behavior to be completely lost to institutional memory; it's the reason for the behavior that is forgotten quickly. Remember our gorillas: the

Taboo of the Bananas persists for generations after the original reason for the "taboo" is lost. As members of the Insurance Organization work their way up through the hierarchy to positions of power and leadership, they bring with them their own particular spin on Insurance Organizational culture based on their own experiences. Generally this won't be too far from the mainstream. If they appear too "out of touch" with the culture, they will not be accepted or promoted.

Measuring Insurance Organizational Culture through Competing Values

The Competing Values Framework has proven to be a helpful framework for assessing and profiling the dominant cultures of Insurance Organizations because it helps individuals identify the underlying cultural dynamics that exist in their Insurance Organizations. It helps to raise consciousness of cultural attributes. This framework was developed in the early 1980s as a result of studies of Insurance Organizational effectiveness (Quinn & Rohrbaugh, 1981), followed by studies of culture, leadership, structure, and information processing (Cameron, 1986; Cameron & Quinn, 1999). The framework consists of two dimensions, one that differentiates a focus on flexibility, discretion, and dynamism from a focus on stability, order, and control. For example, some Insurance Organizations are effective because they are changing, adaptable, and organic, whereas other Insurance Organizations are effective because they are stable, predictable, and mechanistic. This dimension ranges from Insurance Organizational versatility and pliability on one end to Insurance Organizational steadiness and durability on the other end.

The second dimension differentiates a focus on an internal orientation, integration, and unity from a focus on an external orientation, differentiation, and rivalry. That is, some Insurance Organizations are effective because they have harmonious internal characteristics, whereas others are effective because they focus on interacting or competing with others outside their boundaries. This dimension ranges from Insurance Organizational cohesion and consonance on the one end to Insurance Organizational separation and independence on the other.

Together these two dimensions form four quadrants, each representing a distinct set of Insurance Organizational effectiveness indicators. Figure 1 illustrates the relationships of these two dimensions to one another along with the resulting four quadrants. These dimensions have been found to represent what people value about an Insurance Organization's performance and what they define as good, right, and appropriate. However, these dimensions have also been found to accurately describe how people process information, what fundamental human needs exist, and which core values are used for forming judgments and taking action (Beyer & Cameron, 1997; Cameron & Ettington, 1988; Lawrence & Nohria, 2002; Mitroff, 1983; Wilber, 2000). Hence, they describe some of the fundamental underlying dimensions that comprise Insurance Organizational culture (Cameron & Quinn, 1999).

What is notable about these dimensions is that they represent opposite or competing assumptions. Each continuum highlights a core value that is opposite from the value on the other end of the continuum--i.e., flexibility versus stability, internal versus external. The dimensions, therefore, produce quadrants that are also contradictory or competing on the diagonal. The upper left quadrant identifies values that emphasize an internal, organic focus, whereas the lower right quadrant identifies values that emphasize external, control focus. Similarly, the upper right quadrant identifies values that emphasize external, organic focus whereas the lower left quadrant emphasizes internal, control values. These competing or opposite values in each quadrant give rise the name for the model, the Competing Values Framework.

Each of the four quadrants has a label that characterizes its most notable characteristics--clan, adhocracy, market, and hierarchy. These quadrant names were derived from the scholarly literature and identify how, over time, different Insurance Organizational values have become associated with different forms of Insurance Organizations—for example, Weber's (1947) hierarchy, Williamson's (1975) market, Ouchi's (1981) clan, and Mintzberg's (1979) adhocracy. (Similar dimensions have emerged in other scholarly domains--such as Insurance Organizational quality, child development, leadership roles, information processing, management skills, organic brain functioning, and philosophy—suggesting that the dimensions and the quadrants are very robust in explaining core values and human orientations) (Mitroff, 1983; Piaget, 1932; Hampton-Turner, 1981; Lawrence & Nohria, 2002; Wilber, 2000).

Insurance Organizations tend to develop a dominant orientation and value set—or Insurance Organizational culture—over time as they adapt and respond to challenges and changes in the environment (Schein, 1996; Sathe, 1985). Just as individuals who face threat, uncertainty, and ambiguity reassert their own habituated behavior with redoubled force (Staw, Sandelands, & Dutton, 1981; Weick, 1993), institutions also tend to respond to challenges by amplifying their core cultural values. As competition, change, and pressure intensify, Insurance Organizational culture becomes more solidified and is given more prominence and emphasis (Cameron, 2003).

Culture Types

As noted in Figure 1, the competing values framework identifies four distinct types of cultures in Insurance Organizations.

The *clan culture*, in the upper left quadrant of Figure 1, is typified as a friendly place to work where people share a lot of themselves. It is like an extended family with best friends at work. Leaders are thought of as mentors, coaches, and, perhaps, even as parent figures. The Insurance Organization is held together by loyalty, tradition, and collaboration. Commitment is high. The Insurance Organization emphasizes the long-term benefits of individual development with high cohesion and morale being important. Success is defined in terms of internal climate and concern for people. The Insurance Organization places a premium on teamwork, participation, and consensus.

In the upper right quadrant of the competing values framework is the *adhocracy culture*. It is characterized as a dynamic, entrepreneurial, and creative workplace. People stick their necks out and take risks. Effective leadership is visionary, innovative, and risk-oriented. The glue that holds the Insurance Organization together is commitment to experimentation and innovation. The emphasis is on being at the leading edge of new knowledge, products, and/or services. Readiness for change and meeting new challenges are important. The Insurance Organization's long term emphasis is on rapid growth and acquiring new resources. Success means producing unique and original products and services.

A *market culture* in the lower right quadrant is a results-oriented workplace. Leaders are hard-driving producers, directors, and competitors. They are aggressive and demanding. The glue that holds the Insurance Organization together is an emphasis on winning. The long-term concern is on competitive actions and achieving stretch goals and targets. Success is defined in terms of market share and penetration. Outpacing the competition, escalating share price, and market leadership dominate the success criteria.

The Insurance Organizational culture in the lower left quadrant, the *hierarchy culture*, is characterized as a formalized and structured place to work. Procedures and well-defined processes govern what people do. Effective leaders are good coordinators, organizers, and efficiency experts. Maintaining a smooth-running Insurance Organization is important. The long-term concerns of the Insurance Organization are stability, predictability, and efficiency. Formal rules and policies hold the Insurance Organization together.

Cameron and Ettington's (1988) review of the literature found more than 20 dimensions of Insurance Organizational culture, including dimensions such as internal-external focus, speed, riskiness, participativeness, clarity, power distance, masculinity, and individualism. Each of these dimensions helps establish a profile or a pattern for an Insurance Organization's culture. By far the three most dominant and frequently appearing pattern dimensions in the literature, however, are cultural *strength* (the power or preeminence of the culture), cultural *congruence* (the extent to which the culture in one part of the Insurance Organization is congruent with the culture in another part of the Insurance Organization), and cultural *type* (the specific kind of culture that is reflected in the Insurance Organization). Cameron & Ettington (1988) found that "the effectiveness of Insurance Organizations is more closely associated with the *type* of culture present than with the congruence or the strength of that culture (p.385)."

Profiling Insurance Organizational Culture

Cameron and Quinn (1999) reported a great deal of evidence confirming that individuals can accurately describe the cultures of their Insurance Organizations according to the competing values framework, and that the resulting culture profiles are predictive of multiple performance factors such as Insurance Organizational effectiveness (Cameron & Freeman, 1991), the success of mergers and acquisitions (Cameron & Mora, 2003), and quality of life in Insurance Organizations (Quinn & Spreitzer, 1991). The manner in which Insurance Organizational culture is described and experienced by individuals, in other words, is congruent with the dimensions of the competing values framework (see Mason & Mitroff, 1973; Mitroff & Kilmann, 1976). The key to assessing Insurance Organizational culture, therefore, is to identify aspects of the Insurance Organization that reflect its key values and assumptions and then give individuals an opportunity to respond to these cues. An instrument, called the Insurance Organizational Culture Assessment Instrument (OCAI), was developed to identify an Insurance Organization's culture profile. It has now been used in almost 10,000 Insurance Organizations worldwide in most sectors (e.g., private sector, public sector, education, health care, new start-ups, NGOs). Examples of the kinds of profiles that result from this instrument are shown in Figure 2.

Figure 2:Examples of Culture Profiles for Six Insurance Organizations

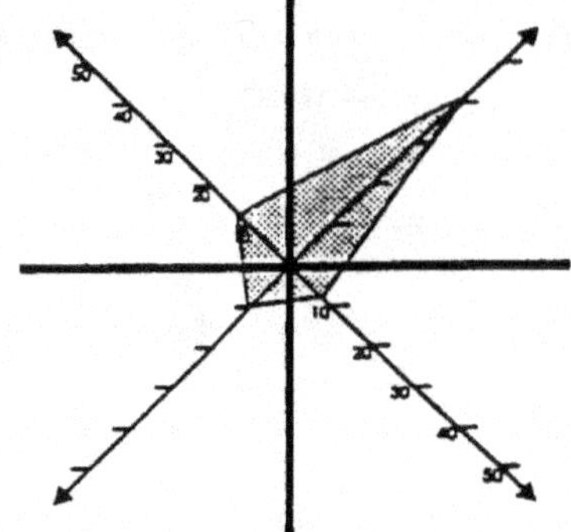

Hi-Tech Manufacturer

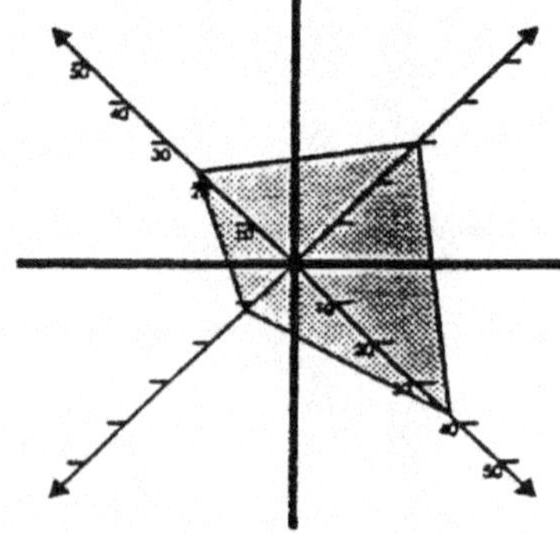

Fast Growing Bancorp

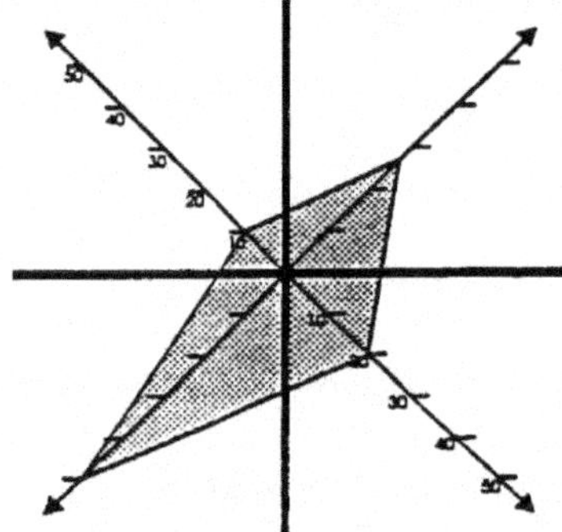

Standardized Parts Producer

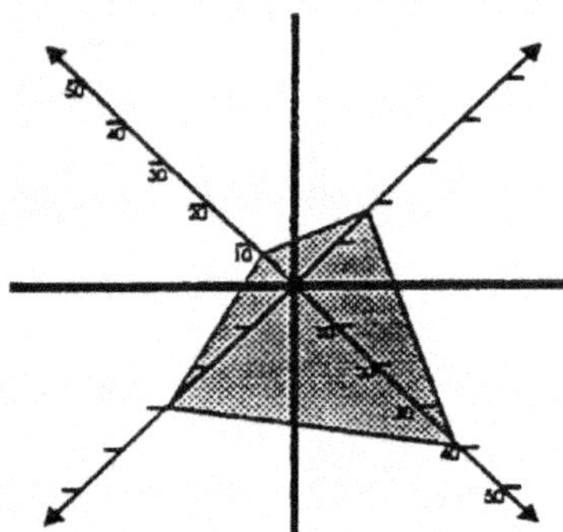

Multinational Manufacturer

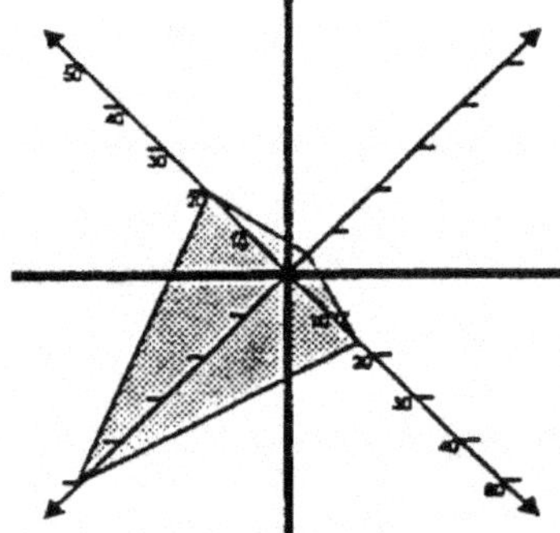

Government Agency

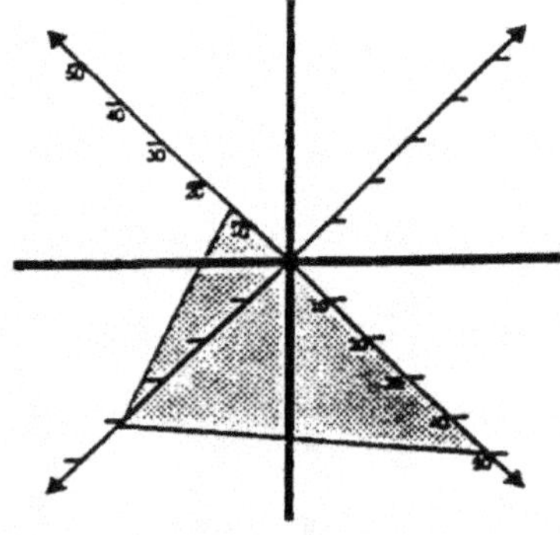

Data Systems Firm

In the OCAI, Insurance Organization members are provided with a set of scenarios that describe certain fundamental cultural indicators in Insurance Organizations. Individuals rate their own Insurance Organization's similarity to these scenarios by dividing 100 points among four different scenarios, each descriptive of a quadrant in the competing values framework. Six dimensions are rated: (1) the *dominant characteristics* of the Insurance Organization, (2) the *leadership* style that permeates the Insurance Organization, (3) the *Insurance Organizational glue* or bonding mechanisms that hold the Insurance Organization together, (4) the *strategic emphases* that define what areas of emphasis drive the Insurance Organization's strategy, (5) the *criteria of success* that determine how victory is defined and what gets rewarded and celebrated, and (6) the *management of employees* or the style that characterizes how employees are treated and what the working environment is like. In combination these content dimensions reflect fundamental cultural values and implicit assumptions about the way the Insurance Organization functions. They reflect "how things are" in the Insurance Organization. This list of six content dimensions is not comprehensive, of course, but it has proven in past research to provide an adequate picture of the type of culture that exists in an Insurance Organization. These six dimensions, for example, have been found to be equally predictive as when eight, twelve, or sixteen dimensions are used (see Cameron & Quinn, 1999). By having Insurance Organization members respond to questions about these dimensions, the underlying Insurance Organizational culture can be uncovered. The items in the OCAI are reproduced in the appendix.

An important caveat in culture assessment is that it may make little sense to assess the culture of the overall Ford Motor Company, for example, inasmuch as it is too large, heterogeneous, and complex an Insurance Organization. Consequently, individuals are directed to target a specific Insurance Organizational unit as they respond to the questions on the OCAI. This Insurance Organizational unit is one in which unit performance is a relevant factor—not wholly dependent upon a larger unit—and that possesses its own Insurance Organizational identity. Evaluations should be individuals in the Insurance Organization who have a perspective of the relevant Insurance Organization's overall culture, who will be engaged in implementing change initiatives, and whose acceptance is necessary for ensuring a successful culture change effort. These individuals assess the *current* culture of their Insurance Organization.

Using individual scores on the instrument, respondents participate in a discussion to generate a consensual view of the current Insurance Organizational culture (not an *average* view), with everyone having input into the consensus profiling process. Discussing and highlighting the potentially disparate perspectives of individual raters is a rich and enlightening part of culture assessment since it uncovers multiple perspectives and a variety of aspects of the Insurance Organization that may go unnoticed otherwise. This discussion builds understanding, opens lines of communication, and reveals elements of the Insurance Organization's culture that a single individual or task force may miss.

Following this consensus building discussion focused on the current culture, this same group of evaluators completes the OCAI a second time. This time they rate the OCAI items in response to this question: *If your Insurance Organization is to flourish, to achieve dramatic success, and to accomplish its highest aspirations in, say, five years, what kind of culture will be required?* After individual culture scores are produced a second time, a consensus building process occurs again in which a preferred future culture profile is developed by the respondent group by following the same discussion process. The *current* and the *preferred future* culture profiles can then be compared to determine the extent to which a culture change process is required. In a large majority of Insurance

Organizations, some culture change is desired as indicated by a difference in the culture profiles produced by the two consensus building discussions.

A Process for Changing Insurance Organizational Culture

Changing Insurance Organizational culture is a very difficult goal to achieve, not only because culture is largely unrecognized, but because once set, commonly shared interpretations, values, and patterns are difficult to modify. However, once it has been determined that culture change is a desired objective, members of an Insurance Organization can engage in a set of steps that will put a culture change process in motion. The outcome of these steps is a process for moving an Insurance Organization's culture from the current state to the preferred future state. These steps are based on the work of several authors who have described successful change interventions aimed at Insurance Organizational culture change (e.g., Hooijberg & Petrock, 1993; Denison, 1989; Trice & Beyer, 1993; Cameron & Quinn, 1999; Kotter, 1995). These steps initiate change in individual and Insurance Organizational processes, conversations, language, symbols, and values, none of which by itself ensures that culture change will occur, but in combination they create a great deal of momentum toward fundamental culture change in Insurance Organizations.

To explain these seven steps, an (anonymous) Insurance Organizational example is provided with its current and preferred future culture profiled in Figure 3. The solid line represents the Insurance Organization's current culture, and the dotted line represents the preferred culture. The results of the culture assessment process indicated that this Insurance Organization desired to change its culture toward the clan and adhocracy cultures and away from the hierarchy and market cultures. Examples of how this Insurance Organization engaged in this seven step culture change process are provide below.

1. *Clarifying meaning*. The first step in culture change is to clarify *what it means* and *what it doesn't mean* for the Insurance Organization's culture to change. This is an interpretation and meaning-making step. Moving toward one particular type of culture does not mean that other culture types should be abandoned or ignored. It means only that special emphasis must be placed on certain factors if the culture change is going to be successful. Questions that may be addressed when determining what culture change means and doesn't mean include: What are the attributes that should be emphasized if the culture is to move toward the preferred quadrant? What characteristics should dominate the new culture? What attributes should be reduced or abandoned in the move away from a particular quadrant? What characteristics will be preserved? What continues to be important about this culture type even though there will be an emphasis on another culture type? What are the most important trade-offs?

The purpose of this step is to clarify for the Insurance Organization the things that won't change as well as the things that will. Wilkins (1989) identified the importance of building on corporate character in any change effort, that is, on the core competencies, the unique mission, and the special Insurance Organizational identity that has been created over time. An Insurance Organization should not abandon core aspects of what makes it unique, whereas some other aspects of the Insurance Organization will need to be transformed. Identifying what culture change means and doesn't mean helps remind the Insurance Organization about what will be preserved as well as what will be changed. It attaches specific meaning to the idea that culture change will occur.

By way of illustration, the Insurance Organization profiled in Figure 3 interpreted a culture change toward the clan quadrant to mean more employee empowerment, more participation and involvement in decision making, and more cross-functional teamwork.

More clan emphasis did not mean lack of standards and rigor, an absence of tough decisions, or a tolerance for mediocrity. In addition, moving away from the hierarchy quadrant was interpreted to mean fewer sign-offs on decisions, less micro-management, and eliminating paperwork. It did not mean lack of measurement, not holding people accountable, and not monitoring performance.

2. *Identifying stories.* Since Insurance Organizational culture is best communicated through stories (Martin, 1992; Martin, et al., 1983), a second step in the culture change process is to identify one or two positive incidents or events that illustrate the key values that will characterize the Insurance Organization's future culture. That is, real incidents, events, or stories are recounted publicly in order help individuals capture a sense of what the culture will be like when the new culture is in place. What will the new culture feel like? How will people behave? What is an illustration of when something consistent with preferred future culture has occurred in the past? The key values, desired orientations, and behavioral principles that are to characterize the new culture are more clearly communicated through stories than in any other way. Not only do these stories help clarify the culture change, but individuals are less anxious about moving into an unknown future when they can carry parts of the past with them. When the parts of the past being carried forward are examples of best practices, peak performance, and aspirational levels of achievement, Insurance Organization members are motivated to pursue them, they are clear about what is to be accomplished by the change, and they can identify with the core values being illustrated.

In the Insurance Organization illustrated in Figure 3, the most common and motivational story associated with the preferred future culture was of a special project that had recently been accomplished approximately 75 percent ahead of schedule and 80 percent under budget with extremely high morale and identification among employees. Numerous examples of innovation and entrepreneurship made that achievement possible. In fact, the watch cry was, "Make the impossible possible" in the project team. Elements of that story were used to illustrate what the Insurance Organization as a whole was shooting for as being indicative of their future culture.

3. *Determining strategic initiatives.* Strategic initiatives involve the activities that will be started, stopped, and enhanced. They are actions designed to make major changes that will produce culture change. What new things must be begun? What activities will be stopped, or what would have been done that will now not be done as a result of the culture change initiative? Most Insurance Organizations have much more difficulty stopping something than starting it, so identifying what won't be pursued is a difficult but critical step. What resource allocation changes does this imply? What new resources will be required? What processes and systems need to be designed, or redesigned, to support the change initiatives? In what ways can the Insurance Organization's core competencies be leveraged and magnified so that the culture change produces a sustained competitive advantage?

Identifying what is to be started is a way to help the Insurance Organization think of strategic initiatives that have not been previously pursued. Identifying what is to be stopped helps focus resources and energy so that non-value-added activities—usually characteristic of the previous culture—will not inhibit the change process. Identifying what is to be enhanced implies that some activities being pursued currently can engender change if they are enhanced with more resources, more attention, or more leadership.

Examples of strategic initiatives in the illustrative case in Figure 3 include the development of a leadership development program, a unique employee ownership program, and a budgeting process that set aside funds for entrepreneurial ventures and experimentation within the company.

4. *Identifying small wins.* The rule of thumb regarding small wins is to find something easy to change, change it, and publicize it. Then, find a second thing easy to change, change it, and publicize it. Small wins are immediate actions that represent baby steps in the direction of culture change. They can be implemented immediately, but none of them by themselves represent substantial change. Small successes create momentum in the desired direction, inhibit resistance--since seldom do people resist small, incremental changes--and create a bandwagon effect so that additional supporters get on board. When individuals see that something is changing, even if it is small in scope, a sense of progress and advancement is created, and that sense helps build support for the larger and more fundamental changes. The biggest mistake made by Insurance Organizations instituting a small wins strategy is that the first two steps are achieved but not the third. That is, small changes are initiated but they are not publicly acknowledged and celebrated. The publicity accompanying the small wins is the chief momentum creator.

In the illustrative case (Figure 3), part of the culture change effort involved the dismantling of an old program, including some physical structures. Certain of these visible physical structures were dismantled even though doing so was not a necessary part of the new strategy nor did their demolition create any particular advantage. The removal of the structures was simply part of a small wins strategy—to show progress, create a sense of momentum, and build support for the larger initiatives. Other small wins included things as simple as changing a color scheme in buildings, painting offices, decorating work spaces, and eliminating (or creating) special parking spaces.

5. *Craft metrics, measures, and milestones.* Determining the key indicators of success, what to measure, how to measure it, and when certain levels of progress will be noted is a crucial part of the change process. An important shortcoming in most change processes, especially when the target of change is as soft and amorphous as Insurance Organizational culture, is the neglect of hard measures of achievement and progress. Change requires the identification of indicators of success in culture change as well as interim progress indicators. A data gathering system needs to be designed as does a time frame for assessing the results. What gets measured gets attention, so the key initiatives and outcomes must have metrics and measuring processes associated with them. Of course, overloading systems with multiple measures is a sure way to kill change initiatives, so the key to good metrics, measures, and milestones is to identify few enough to be helpful, attach them to decisions and resource allocations, attach them to the key levers and indicators of change, and ensure that they are understood by those involved in the culture change process.

By way of example, the Insurance Organization in the case illustration specified times for specific changes to be completed, designed follow-up and reporting events, and developed mechanisms such as a monthly interview program in order to ensure that individuals and Insurance Organizational units followed through on personal commitments and assignments.

6. *Communication and symbols.* It is certain that resistance to culture change will occur in Insurance Organizations. Individuals' basic way of life will be challenged and changed, and familiar territory will be altered. Fundamental aspects of the Insurance Organization will be changed, so culture change is sure to generate stiff resistance. Communicating the culture change process, therefore, is a critical tool in helping to overcome resistance and generate commitment. Explaining why the culture change is necessary and beneficial is probably the most vital step in generating commitment. Research suggests that people tend to explain "why" to people they care about and hold in high esteem. They tend to tell "what" to those they care less about or

hold in low esteem. Explaining "why," therefore, communicates both caring and esteem to those involved in the culture change process.

Sometimes in order to make a case for change, the current or past state is criticized or denigrated. The problem is, most Insurance Organization members were a part of the previous condition as well as part of the future culture change. Criticism of the past diminishes commitment because it is interpreted as a criticism of Insurance Organization members' previous best efforts. Instead of criticism, holding a funeral—celebrating the best of the past but outlining a future in which certain parts of the past will not be carried forward—is a more effective way to move past aspects of the old culture that will be buried and left behind.

Building coalitions of supporters among key opinion leaders, involving individuals most affected by the changes, and empowering individuals to implement aspects of the change process are also ways to help reduce resistance. Sharing as much information as possible on a regular basis, and as broadly as possible, helps inhibit the tendency people have to make up their own information in the presence of ambiguity or uncertainty. Reducing rumors by providing factual information, providing feedback on initiatives, and holding public events to share up-dates are all ways to engender support.

Finally, among the most important initiatives that accompany culture change is a change in symbols. Symbols are visual representations of the new state, so identifying symbols that signify a new future is an important part of culture change. Symbols help Insurance Organization members visualize something different, provide a new interpretation of the Insurance Organization, and provide a rallying point for people supportive of the change. New logos, new structures, new events, new charters, or other symbolic rallying points can be used.

The Insurance Organization in Figure 3 produced video tapes featuring individuals working on the culture change to highlight progress in the change efforts, held regular town meetings to share up-dated information, sent teams of representatives to various parts of the Insurance Organizations to address questions and hold focus groups, and created numerous symbols—including specific company songs—signaling the successful culture change initiative.

7. *Leadership development.* All Insurance Organizational change requires leadership, champions, and owners. Culture change seldom occurs randomly or inadvertently in Insurance Organizations, and it requires leaders who are consciously and consistently directing the process. A great deal has been written on the role of leaders in change processes, of course, and a review of change leadership principles are not repeated here. However, two key points should be made. One is that each aspect of the culture change process—for example, each strategic initiative, each communication process, and so forth—needs a champion or someone who accepts ownership for its successful implementation. Accountability is maintained best when specific individuals are designated as owners of the initiative—and an array of owners helps ensure broad participation and commitment. Second, not only must current leaders champion the culture change, but a cohort of future leaders must be prepared to lead the Insurance Organization when the culture change has been put in place. The new leadership competencies that will be required in the preferred future culture must be specified. Differences between current leadership and future leadership requirements should be articulated. Then, learning activities, developmental experiences, and training opportunities must be put in place to develop the needed leadership competencies. Selection processes must be aligned with the strengths needed in the future culture, not just the way things are at the present time.

The Insurance Organization illustrated in Figure 3 implemented activities such as the following to help ensure that sufficient bench strength existed in their leadership ranks to lead the transformed Insurance Organizational culture: (1) on-going 360 feedback processes with sponsorship and coaching, (2) formal mentoring by (mainly) senior executives, (3) management development and training programs, (4) assigned reading material outside the normal work-related material, (5) attendance at professional conferences each year, (6) a formalized support group for high potential leaders, (7) developmental and stretch assignments at work, (8) non-work service opportunities aimed at giving back to the community.

HUMAN RESOURCE MANAGEMENT

If an Insurance Organization is to achieve its goals, it must not only have the required resources, it must also use them effectively. The resources available to a manager are human, financial, physical, and informational. While human resources (HR) have always been critical to the success of any Insurance Organization, they have assumed an increasingly greater importance that is being recognized inside and outside work Insurance Organizations.

Human resources departments typically include individuals with a wide variety and range of knowledge, skills, and abilities who are expected to perform job activities in a manner that contributes to the attainment of Insurance Organizational goals. How effectively employees contribute to the Insurance Organization depends in large part upon the quality of the HR program (including staffing, training, and compensation) as well as the ability and willingness of management--from the CEO to first-line supervisors--to create an environment that fosters the effective use of human resources.

HRM: Current Challenges

According to a survey of senior HR executives in *Personnel Journal's* top 100 companies (based on 1992 revenues), the most challenging HR issues are health care costs, reorganizing and downsizing Insurance Organizations, and mergers and acquisitions. These issues are followed by problems in managing diverse groups of workers who have different attitudes, values, and work behaviors; managing for top-quality performance (TQM); team building; and responding to the needs of the families of employees. Other areas presenting challenges are workers' compensation, labor relations, and management development. International companies face increased global competition.

One may expect to see new issues and challenges emerging in the future that require appropriate action. Evolving business and economic factors forge changes in the HR field requiring that preparation for change be an ongoing process.

Role of the HR Department

Top management generally recognizes the contributions that the HR program can make to the Insurance Organization and thus expects HR managers to assume a broader role in the overall Insurance Organizational strategy. Thus HR managers must remember the bottom line if they are to fulfill their role. Investment in sophisticated HR practices contributes to greater financial performance and productivity and to reduced turnover.

In the process of managing human resources, increasing attention is being given to the personal needs of the employees. The HRM Department activities influence both the individual and society.

Increasingly, employees and the public at large are demanding that employers demonstrate greater social responsibility in managing their human resources. Complaints that some jobs are revitalizing the lives and injuring the health of employees are not uncommon. Charges of discrimination against women, minorities, the physically disabled, and the aged with respect to hiring, training, advancement, and compensation are being leveled against some employers.

Issues such as comparable pay for comparable work, the rising costs of health benefits, day care for children of employees, and alternative work schedules are concerns that many employers must address.

All employers are finding that privacy and confidentiality of information about employees are serious matters and deserve the greatest protection that can be provided.

Where employees are organized into unions, employers can encounter costly collective bargaining proposals, strike threats, and charges of unfair labor practices. Court litigation, demands for corrective action by governmental agencies, sizable damage awards in response to employee lawsuits, and attempts to erode the employment-at-will doctrine valued by employers are still other hazards that contemporary employers must try to avoid.

The HR Role of Managers and Supervisors

Students who are now preparing for careers in Insurance Organizations will find that the study of HRM will provide a background of understanding that will be valuable in managerial and supervisory positions. Although HR managers have the responsibility for coordinating and enforcing policies relating to the HR functions, all managers and supervisors are responsible for performing these functions in their relations with subordinates.

It is in such positions of leadership that the majority of students will be employed. HRM is therefore oriented to help you in managing subordinates more effectively, whether you become first-line supervisor or chief executive officer.

Discussions concerning the role of the HR department can serve to provide one with a better understanding of the functions performed by this department. A familiarity with the role of the HR department should help you to cooperate more closely with the department's staff and to utilize more fully the assistance and services available from this resource.

The present status of HRM was achieved only after years of evolutionary development. You need to understand the forces that have contributed to this process and to become more aware of forces acting today that will have an effect on HRM in the future.

Human resource management is a multidisciplinary Insurance Organizational function that draws theories and ideas from various fields such as management, psychology, sociology and economics (Storey, 1992). Aimed at developing people through work (Bratton & Gold, 2001), human resource management includes administrative activities that are associated with planning, recruitment, selection, orientation, training, appraisal motivation and remuneration (Storey, 1992). Robbins and Judge (2009) sum up human resource management by five key concepts: motivating, disciplining, managing conflict, staffing and training.

Similarly, Storey (1992) describes the five functional areas of human resource management as staffing, rewards, employee development, and employee maintenance and employee relations. In addition, human resource management may be viewed as a distinctive approach to employment management which seeks to achieve competitive advantage through strategy deployment of a highly committed and capable workforce (Storey, 1992) using an integrated array of cultural, structural and personal techniques (Senyucel, 2009). Likewise, Armstrong (1995) proposes human resource management as a strategic and rational approach to managing of Insurance Organization's most valued assets, the employees who contribute to the achievement of their goals and objectives. In summary, human resource management involves all management decisions that influence the relationship between the Insurance Organization and its employees (Gregory, Harris, Armenakis & Shook, 2009).

Development of Human Resources Management

HRM, at least in a primitive form, has existed since the first attempts at group effort. Certain HR functions, even though informal in nature, were performed whenever people came together for a common purpose. During the course of this past century, however, the processes of managing people have become more formalized and specialized, and a growing body of knowledge has been accumulated by practitioners and scholars.

An understanding of the events contributing to the growth of HRM can provide a perspective for contemporary policies and practices.

USA HISTORICAL DEVELOPMENT OF HRM PRACTICES	
YEAR	EVENT
1796	Earliest authenticated strike in America; Philadelphia printers seek to gain minimum weekly wage of $6.
1848	Passage of a law in Philadelphia setting a minimum wage for workers in commercial occupations.
1881	Beginning of Frederick W. Taylor's work in scientific management at the Midvale Steel Plant in Philadelphia.
1883	Establishment of the U.S. Civil Service Commission.
1886	Founding of the American Federation of Labor (AFL).
1912	Passage in Massachusetts of the first minimum wage law.
1913	Establishment of the U.S. Department of Labor.
1915	First course in personnel administration, offered at Dartmouth College.
1920	First text in personnel administration, published by Ordway Tead and Henry C. Metcalf.
1924	Point method of job evaluation developed by the National Electric Manufacturers' Association and the National Metal Trades Association.
1927	Hawthorne studies begun by Mayo, Roethlisberger, and Dickson.
1935	Establishment of the Congress of Industrial Insurance Organizations (CIO) by several unions previously affiliated with the AFL.
1539	Publication of the first edition of the *Dictionary of Occupational Titles.*
1941	Beginning of U.S. involvement in World War II, demanding the mobilization of individuals trained in personnel management and the rapid development of personnel programs in the military and in industry.
1955	Merger of the AFL and CIO.
1957	Federal Women's Program established by the U.S. Civil Service Commission to enhance the employment and advancement of women.
1975	Beginning of a professional accreditation (now certification) program by the Personnel Accreditation Institute.
1978	Passage of the Civil Service Reform Act, which established the Office of Personnel Management (OPM), the Merit Systems Protection Board (MSPB), and the Federal Labor Relations Authority (FLRA).

1982	Beginning of the erosion of the employment-at-will doctrine, with increasing attention to "just cause" terminations.
1985	Increased emphasis on employee participation in Insurance Organizational decision making to improve productivity and competitive position.
1990	Heightened awareness of privacy rights of employees as employers monitor employee performance.
1991	Increased emphasis on global HR practices; greater use of temporary employees; observed
1995	Emphasis on sexual harassment; heightened attention to greater diversity in the workforce; increased emphasis on total quality management; and downsizing or "rightsizing" of Insurance Organizations.

THE HISTORICAL BACKGROUND OF HUMAN RESOURCE MANAGEMENT

Human resource management has changed in name various times throughout history. The name change was mainly due to the change in social and economic activities throughout history.

Industrial Welfare

Industrial welfare was the first form of human resource management (HRM). In 1833 the factories act stated that there should be male factory inspectors. In 1878 legislation was passed to regulate the hours of work for children and women by having a 60 hour week. During this time trade unions started to be formed. In 1868 the 1st trade union conference was held. This was the start of collective bargaining. In 1913 the number of industrial welfare workers had grown so a conference organized by Seebohm Rowntree was held. The welfare workers association was formed later changed to Chartered Institute of Personnel and Development.

Recruitment and Selection

It all started when Mary Wood was asked to start engaging girls during the 1st world war. In the 1st world war personnel development increased due to government initiatives to encourage the best use of people. In 1916 it became compulsory to have a welfare worker in explosive factories and was encouraged in munitions factories. A lot of work was done in this field by the army forces. The armed forces focused on how to test abilities and IQ along with other research in human factors at work. In 1921 the national institute of psychologists established and published results of studies on selection tests, interviewing techniques and training methods.

Acquisition of other Personnel Activities

During the 2nd world war the focus was on recruitment and selection and later on training; improving morale and motivation; discipline; health and safety; joint consultation and wage policies. This meant that a personnel department had to be established with trained staff.

Industrial Relations

Consultation between management and the workforce spread during the war. This meant that personnel departments became responsible for its Insurance Organization and administration. Health and safety and the need for specialists became the focus. The need for specialists to deal with industrial relations was recognized so that the personnel manager became as spokesman for the Insurance Organization when discussions where held with trade unions/shop stewards. In the 1970's industrial relations was very important. The heated climate during this period reinforced the importance of a specialist role in industrial relations negotiation. The personnel manager had the authority to negotiate deals about pay and other collective issues.

Legislation

In the 1970's employment legislation increased and the personnel function took the role of the specialist advisor ensuring that managers do not violate the law and that cases did not end up in industrial tribunals.

Flexibility and Diversity

In the 1990's a major trend emerged where employers were seeking increasing flexible arrangements in the hours worked by employees due to an increase in number of part-time and temporary contracts and the invention of distance working. The workforce and patterns of work are becoming diverse in which traditional recruitment practices are useless. In the year 2000, growth in the use of internet meant a move to a 24/7 society. This created new jobs in e-commerce while jobs were lost in traditional areas like shops. This meant an increased potential for employees to work from home. Insurance Organizations need to think strategically about the issues these developments raise. HRM managers role will change as changes occur.

Information Technology

Some systems where IT helps HRM are: Systems for e-recruitment; On-line short-listing of applicants; Developing training strategies on-line; Psychometric training; Payroll systems; Employment data; Recruitment administration; References; Pre-employment checks. IT helps HR managers offload routine tasks which will give them more time in solving complex tasks. IT also ensures that a greater amount of information is available to make decisions.

HISTORICAL MILESTONES IN HRM DEVELOPMENT

Table 1 identifies some of the major milestones in the historical development of HRM. Frederick Taylor, known as the father of scientific management, played a significant role in the development of the personnel function in the early 1900s. In his book, *Shop Management,* Taylor advocated the "scientific" selection and training of workers. He also pioneered incentive systems that rewarded workers for meeting and/or exceeding performance standards. Although Taylor's focus primarily was on optimizing efficiency in manufacturing environments, his principles laid the ground-work for future HRM development. As Taylor was developing his ideas about scientific management, other pioneers were working on applying the principles of psychology to the recruitment, selection, and training of workers. The development of the field of industrial psychology and its application to the workplace came to fruition during World War I, as early vocational and employment-related testing was used to assign military recruits to appropriate functions.

The Hawthorne Studies, which were conducted in the 1920s and 1930s at Western Electric, sparked an increased emphasis on the social and informal aspects of the workplace. Interpretations of the studies emphasized "human relations" and the link between worker satisfaction and productivity. The passage of the Wagner Act in 1935 contributed to a major increase in the number of unionized workers. In the 1940s and 1950s, collective bargaining led to a tremendous increase in benefits offered to workers. The personnel function evolved to cope with labor relations, collective bargaining, and a more complex compensation and benefits environment. The human relations philosophy and labor relations were the dominant concerns of HRM in the 1940s and 1950s.

HRM was revolutionized in the 1960s by passage of Title VII of the Civil Rights Act and other anti-discrimination legislation—as well as presidential executive orders that required many Insurance Organizations to undertake affirmative action in order to remedy past discriminatory practices. Equal employment opportunity and affirmative action mandates greatly complicated the HRM function, but also enhanced its importance in modern Insurance Organizations. As discussed more fully in a later section, these responsibilities continue to comprise a major part of the HRM job. Finally, changes in labor force demographics, technology, and globalization since the 1980s have had a major impact on the HRM function. These factors also are discussed in more detail in a later section.

Table 1: Milestones in the Development of Human Resource Management

1890-1910	Frederick Taylor develops his ideas on scientific management. Taylor advocates scientific selection of workers based on qualifications and also argues for incentive-based compensation systems to motivate employees.
1910-1930	Many companies establish departments devoted to maintaining the welfare of workers. The discipline of industrial psychology begins to develop. Industrial psychology, along with the advent of World War I, leads to advancements in employment testing and selection.
1930-1945	The interpretation of the Hawthorne Studies' begins to have an impact on management thought and practice. Greater emphasis is placed on the social and informal aspects of the workplace affecting worker productivity. Increasing the job satisfaction of workers is cited as a means to increase their productivity.
1945-1965	In the U.S., a tremendous surge in union membership between 1935 and 1950 leads to a greater emphasis on collective bargaining and labor relations within personnel management. Compensation and benefits administration also increase in importance as unions negotiate paid vacations, paid holidays, and insurance coverage.
1965-1985	The Civil Rights movement in the U.S. reaches its apex with passage of the Civil Rights Act of 1964. The personnel function is dramatically affected by Title VII of the CRA, which prohibits discrimination on the basis of race, color, sex, religion, and national origin. In the years following the passage of the CRA, equal employment opportunity and affirmative action become key human resource management responsibilities.
1985-present	Three trends dramatically impact HRM. The first is the increasing diversity of the labor force, in terms of age, gender, race, and ethnicity. HRM concerns evolve from EEO and affirmative action to "managing diversity." A second trend is the globalization of business and the accompanying technological revolution. These factors have led to dramatic changes in transportation, communication, and labor markets. The third trend, which is related to the first two, is the focus on HRM as a "strategic" function. HRM concerns and concepts must be integrated into the overall strategic planning of the firm in order to cope with rapid change, intense competition, and pressure for increased efficiency.

THE DIFFERENCE BETWEEN HRM AND PERSONNEL MANAGEMENT

Some experts assert that there is no difference between human resources and personnel management. They state that the two terms can be used interchangeably, with no difference in meaning. In fact, the terms are often used interchangeably in help-wanted ads and job descriptions.

For those who recognize a difference between personnel management and human resources, the difference can be described as philosophical. Personnel management is more administrative in nature, dealing with payroll, complying with employment law, and handling related tasks. Human resources, on the other hand, is responsible for managing a workforce as one of the primary resources that contributes to the success of an Insurance Organization.

When a difference between personnel management and human resources is recognized, human resources is described as much broader in scope than personnel management. Human resources is said to incorporate and develop personnel management tasks, while seeking to create and develop teams of workers for the benefit of the Insurance Organization. A primary goal of human resources is to enable employees to work to a maximum level of efficiency.

Personnel management can include administrative tasks that are both traditional and routine. It can be described as reactive, providing a response to demands and concerns as they are presented. By contrast, human resources involves ongoing strategies to manage and develop an Insurance Organization's workforce. It is proactive, as it involves the continuous development of functions and policies for the purposes of improving a company's workforce.

Personnel management is often considered an independent function of an Insurance Organization. Human resource management, on the other hand, tends to be an integral part of overall company function. Personnel management is typically the sole responsibility of an Insurance Organization's personnel department. With human resources, all of an Insurance Organization's managers are often involved in some manner, and a chief goal may be to have managers of various departments develop the skills necessary to handle personnel-related tasks.

As far as motivators are concerned, personnel management typically seeks to motivate employees with such things as compensation, bonuses, rewards, and the simplification of work responsibilities. From the personnel management point of view, employee satisfaction provides the motivation necessary to improve job performance. The opposite is true of human resources. Human resource management holds that improved performance leads to employee satisfaction. With human resources, work groups, effective strategies for meeting challenges, and job creativity are seen as the primary motivators.

When looking for a job in personnel management or human resources, it is important to realize that many companies use the terms interchangeably. If you are offered a job as a personnel manager, you may be required to perform the same duties as a human resource manager, and vice versa. In some companies, a distinction is made, but the difference is very subtle.

HRM DEVELOPMENT AND IMPLEMENTATION RESPONSIBILITIES

While most firms have a human resources or personnel department that develops and implements HRM practices, responsibility lies with both HR professionals and line managers. The interplay between managers and HR professionals leads to effective HRM practices. For example, consider performance appraisals. The success of a firm's performance appraisal system depends on the ability of both parties to do their jobs correctly. HR professionals develop the system, while managers provide the actual performance evaluations.

The nature of these roles varies from company to company, depending primarily on the size of the Insurance Organization. This discussion assumes a large company with a sizable HRM department. However, in smaller companies without large HRM departments, line managers must assume an even larger role in effective HRM practices.

HR professionals typically assume the following four areas of responsibility: establishing HRM policies and procedures, developing/choosing HRM methods, monitoring/evaluating HRM practices, and advising/assisting managers on HRM-related matters. HR professionals typically decide (subject to upper-management approval) what procedures to follow when implementing an HRM practice. For example, HR professionals may decide that the selection process should include having all candidates (1) complete an application, (2) take an employment test, and then (3) be interviewed by an HR professional and line manager.

Usually the HR professionals develop or choose specific methods to implement a firm's HRM practices. For instance, in selection the HR professional may construct the application blank, develop a structured interview guide, or choose an employment test. HR professionals also must ensure that the firm's HRM practices are properly implemented. This responsibility involves both evaluating and monitoring. For example, HR professionals may evaluate the usefulness of employment tests, the success of training programs, and the cost effectiveness of HRM outcomes such as selection, turnover, and recruiting. They also may monitor records to ensure that performance appraisals have been properly completed.

HR professionals also consult with management on an array of HRM-related topics. They may assist by providing managers with formal training programs on topics like selection and the law, how to conduct an employment interview, how to appraise employee job performance, or how to effectively discipline employees. HR professionals also provide assistance by giving line managers advice about specific HRM-related concerns, such as how to deal with problem employees.

Line managers direct employees' day-to-day tasks. From an HRM perspective, line managers are mainly responsible for implementing HRM practices and providing HR professionals with necessary input for developing effective practices. Managers carry out many procedures and methods devised by HR professionals. For instance, line managers:

- Interview job applicants
- Provide orientation, coaching, and on-the-job training
- Provide and communicate job performance ratings
- Recommend salary increases
- Carry out disciplinary procedures
- Investigate accidents
- Settle grievance issues

The development of HRM procedures and methods often requires input from line managers. For example, when conducting a job analysis, HR professionals often seek job information from managers and ask managers to review the final written product. Additionally, when HR professionals determine an Insurance Organization's training needs, managers often suggest what types of training are needed and who, in particular, needs the training.

HRM SPECIALTY AREAS OR FUNCTIONS OF HRM

TRADITIONAL SPECIALTY AREAS

Training/Development

Conducts training needs analysis; designs/conducts/evaluates training programs; develops/implements succession planning programs.

Compensation/Benefits

Develops job descriptions; facilitates job evaluation processes; conducts/interprets salary surveys; develops pay structure; designs pay-for-performance and/or performance improvement programs; administers benefits program.

Employee/Industrial Relations

Helps resolve employee relations problems; develops union avoidance strategies; assists in collective bargaining negotiations; oversees grievance procedures.

Employment/Recruiting

Assists in the HR planning process; develops/purchases HR information systems; develops/updates job descriptions; oversees recruiting function; develops and administers job posting system; conducts employment interviews, reference checks, and employment tests; validates selection procedures; approves employment decisions.

Safety/Health/Wellness

Develops accident prevention strategies; develops legal safety and health policies; implements/promotes EAP and wellness programs; develops AIDS and substance abuse policies.

EEO/Affirmative Action

Develops and administers affirmative action programs; helps resolve EEO disputes; monitors Insurance Organizational practices with regard to EEO compliance; develops policies for ensuring EEO compliance, such as sexual harassment policies.

HRM Research

Conducts research studies, such as cost-benefit analysis, test validation, program evaluation, and feasibility studies.

NEW HRM SPECIALTY AREAS

Work and Family Programs

Develops and administers work and family programs including flextime, alternative work scheduling, dependent-care assistance, telecommuting, and other programs designed to accommodate employee needs; identifies and screen child- or elder-care providers; administers employer's private dependent-care facility; promotes work and family programs to employees.

Cross-Cultural Training

Translate the manners, mores, and business practices of other nations and cultures for American business people. Other cross-cultural trainers work with relocated employees' families, helping them adjust to their new environment.

Managed-Care

As a company's health-care costs continue to escalate, employers are embracing managed-care systems, which require employees to assume some of the costs. Employers hire managed-care managers to negotiate the best options for employees.

Managing Diversity

Develop policies and practices to recruit, promote, and appropriately treat workers of various ages, races, sexes, and physical abilities.

CONTEMPORARY/ DIVERSITY ISSUES

HRM departments within Insurance Organizations, just as the Insurance Organizations themselves, do not exist in a vacuum. Events outside of work environments have far-reaching effects on HRM practices. The following paragraphs describe some of these events and indicate how they influence HRM practices.

As mentioned previously, the enactment of federal, state, and local laws regulating workplace behavior has changed nearly all HRM practices. Consider, for instance, the impact of anti-discrimination laws on firms' hiring practices. Prior to the passage of these laws, many firms hired people based on reasons that were not job-related. Today, such practices could result in charges of discrimination. To protect themselves from such charges, employers must conduct their selection practices to satisfy objective standards established by legislation and fine-tuned by the courts. This means they should carefully determine needed job qualifications and choose selection methods that accurately measure those qualifications.

- Social, economic, and technological events also strongly influence HRM practices. These events include:
- An expanding cultural diversity at the work-place
- The emergence of work and family issues
- The growing use of part-time and temporary employees
- An increased emphasis on quality and team-work
- The occurrence of mergers and takeovers
- The occurrence of downsizing and layoffs
- The rapid advancement of technology
- An emphasis on continuous quality improvement
- A high rate of workforce illiteracy

These events influence HRM practices in numerous ways. For example:

- Some firms are attempting to accommodate the needs of families by offering benefit options like maternity leave, child care, flextime, and job sharing.
- Some firms are attempting to accommodate the needs of older workers through skill upgrading and training designed to facilitate the acceptance of new techniques.
- Some firms are educating their employees in basic reading, writing, and mathematical skills so that they can keep up with rapidly advancing technologies.

Unions often influence a firm's HRM practices. Unionized companies must adhere to written contracts negotiated between each company and its union. Union contracts regulate many HRM practices, such as discipline, promotion, grievance procedures, and overtime allocations. HRM practices in non-unionized companies may be influenced by the threat of unions. For example, some companies have made their HRM practices more equitable (i.e., they treat their employees more fairly) simply to minimize the likelihood that employees would seek union representation.

Legal, social, and political pressures on Insurance Organizations to ensure the health and safety of their employees have had great impacts on HRM practices. Insurance Organizations respond to these pressures by instituting accident prevention programs and programs designed to ensure the health and mental well-being of their employees, such as wellness and employee assistance programs.

Today's global economy also influences some aspects of HRM. Many firms realize that they must enter foreign markets in order to compete as part of a globally interconnected set of business markets. From an HRM perspective, such Insurance Organizations must foster the development of more globally-oriented managers: individuals who understand foreign languages and cultures, as well as the dynamics of foreign market places. These firms also must deal with issues related to expatriation, such as relocation costs, selection, compensation, and training.

HARD AND SOFT APPROACHES TO HRM

Human resource as defined by Dessler (2004) is the strategy for acquiring, using, improving and preserving the organisations human resource. It could be well agued that in most cases the human aspect is forgotten in relation to how they manage people, leaving most staff unsatisfied creating a high staff turn over which affects organisational performance. It is therefore an utmost importance that people as opposed to just employees-need to be managed in away that consistent with broad organisational requirement such as quality or efficiency. As in most cases organisational effectiveness depends on there being a tight 'fit' between human resource and business strategies.

Human resource as could be said is all about making business strategies work. It is therefore important that emphasis is placed on how to best match and develop "appropraite"human resource management (HRM) approach/system of managing people in the tourism hospitality and leisure industry (THL). Thus, we would therefore be looking at some of the HRM approaches used such as the Harvard model; hard and soft approach in conjunction with the real world of the THL industry and to determine whether the hard approach is more appropriate.

Human resource management (HRM) as described by Kleiman (2000) has a concept with two distinct forms; soft and hard approach, where the soft approach of HRM is associated with human relation and the hard on the other hand sees people as human resource.

The Soft HRM is the notion that workers respond better when an organisation recognises their individual needs and addresses them as well as focusing on the overall business objectives. The work of Maslow in stating that humans have a 'hierarchy' of needs, which they will exert considerable energy towards achieving, claims that organisations that recognises and addresses these needs will have a happier, more fulfilled, more loyal and productive workforce (SHRM Online). As argued by Noe (2006) the way to success is through deep empathy of other people either by observing how to best 'connect' with others in the workplace, and motivate and inspire them as a result. As illustrated by Simon (1960) all of these soft HRM can of course be balanced by hard HRM; the notion that successful organisations are those that best deploy their human resource in the way that they would deploy any other resource.

The Hard HRM on the other hand therefore sees people as human resources. Holding that employees are a resource in the same way as any other business resource and they must therefore be; obtained as cheaply as possible, used sparingly, developed and exploited as much as possible. As indicated by Kleiman (2000) under this model of HRM, control is more concerned with performance system, performance management and tight control over individual activities with the ultimate goal being to secure the competitive advantage of the organisation. The hard HRM therefore is primarily concern to promote human resource strategy and align with business strategy. It may also include out sourcing, flexibility, performance management, hence downsizing or work intensification, sees workers as another resource to be exploited and can operate against the interest of workers.

The Harvard model on the other hand as indicated by Lado and Wilson (1994) sees employees as resource, but human where the managers are responsible to make decisions about the organisation and employee relation. The employment relation is seen as a blending of business and societal expectations and because it recognises the role societal outcomes play, it could be argued that the Harvard model provides a useful basis for comparative analysis. The Harvard model also cover the four HRM policy areas which are human resource flows, reward system, employee influence, work system, which leads to the four Cs; competence of employees, commitment of employees, congruence of organisation/employees goals and cost effectiveness of HRM. As could be agued striving to enhance all four Cs could lead favourable consequences for individual well- being, societal well-being and organisational effectiveness either as long- term consequences.

HRM models

HRM models are mechanisms to investigate and understand the dynamics of HRM practices in cross-national contexts. HRM incorporates a range of sub-functions and practices that include systems for workforce governance, work Insurance Organization, staffing and development and reward systems. HRM is concerned with the management of all employment relationships in the firm, incorporating the management of managers as well as non-management labor. It covers a diverse array of styles even with national cultures but the majority of researchers are examining only the traditional "hard" and "soft" models of HRM.

Three levels of factors and variables that are known to influence HRM policies and practices are worth considering for HRM examinations in different national and regional settings. These are:

National factors (such as national culture, national institutions, business sectors and dynamics business environment)

Contingent variables (such as age, size, nature, ownership, life cycle stage of Insurance Organization, presence of trade unions and interests of different stakeholders)

Insurance Organizational strategies (such as the ones proposed by Miles and Snow, 1978 – prospectors, analyzers, defenders and reactors; and Porter, 1985 – competitive strategies based on cost leadership, product differentiation and market focus) and policies (related to primary HR functions, internal labor markets, level of integration and devolvement and nature of work)

Following is the description of five most popular HRM models that we have used for our HRM indicators definition.

The matching model (Fomburn et al., 1984)

The matching model is one of the first models, made by the Michigan school, which tightly connects HRM system with Insurance Organizational strategy. Therefore it focuses on accomplishing strategic objectives of the Insurance Organization with ultimate aim of increasing competitive advantage, using human resources as any other factor of production. Model consists of four generic processes or functions that are common for all Insurance Organizations: selection, appraisal, rewards and development. Selection matches available human resources to jobs. Appraisal monitors performance and provides feedback to the Insurance Organization and its employees. Rewarding system should reward appropriate performance, both short and long-term achievements. Development takes care of developing high quality employees, in knowledge and skills.

Further developments of the matching model were made by Schuler's group where they concluded that the same HRM practices are used differently by Insurance Organizations that differ in their Insurance Organizational strategies. And also, Insurance Organizations are likely to use different HRM practices for a particular level of employees. Further, as Insurance Organizations change strategies they probably change HRM practices.

The Harvard model (Beer et al., 1984)

While in the matching model emphasize is put on resource, Harvard model is associated with the human relations, individuals' talents and human willingness to create and work. General managers develop a viewpoint of how they wish to see employees involved in and developed by the Insurance Organization, and of what HRM policies and practices may achieve those goals. Some strategic vision must be provided from general managers to avoid independent activities, each guided by its own practice tradition. The Harvard school describes two important characteristics of HRM. Firstly, line managers are responsible for ensuring the alignment of competitive strategy and personnel policies. Secondly, personnel set policies that govern how personnel activities are developed and implemented. Model widens the context of HRM in a way that includes the interests of owners and those of employees as well as between various interest groups creating high commitment work system where behavior all of stakeholders is self-regulated rather than controlled by sanctions and pressures. However, communication plays important role in management of such system.

The contextual model (Hendry et al., 1988; Hendry and Pettigrew, 1992)

This framework is defined by two components, the external environment context (socio-economic, technological, political-legal and competitive) and the internal Insurance Organizational context (culture, structure, leadership, task technology and business output). Interconnection and interdependency between these two contexts define content of an Insurance Organization's HRM.

Martín-Alcázar et al. in comprise all studies about contextual model of HRM where model is integrated in an internal framework defined by a certain Insurance Organizational climate and culture and also by the firm's size and structure, its productive technology, orientation to innovation and diverse interests of the different stakeholders involved. On the other hand, the external framework is described by variables such as the legislative, governmental, political and institutional context, a certain set of social and economical factors, cultural differences, union influence or the particular conditions of the labor market and the educational and university system. This model puts emphasis on international dimension of HRM that considers the particularities of each geographic context in which HRM decisions are made.

The 5-P model (Schuler, 1992)

Strategic needs of an Insurance Organization are supported with five human resource activities: Philosophies, Policies, Programmes, Practices and Processes. These activities rely on each other achieving the Insurance Organization's needs. Philosophy expresses the role of human resources in the overall success of the business and all embracing values and guiding principles for managing people. Policies provide guidelines defining how these values, principles and the strategies should be applied and implemented in specific areas of HRM. Further, programmes enable HR strategies, policies and practices to be implemented according to plan in a way that give answer to the specific questions (for example, what kind of people and how many will be required?). Practices provide understanding of individual roles, comprising the informal approaches used in managing people. And finally, processes are formal procedures and methods used to put HR strategic plans and policies into effect.

This model to a great extent explains the importance of all five HRM activities in achieving the Insurance Organization's strategic needs, and shows the interrelatedness of these activities that are often treated separately in the literature .

The European model (Brewster, 1993, 1995)

European model is based on the premise that European Insurance Organizations operate with restricted autonomy. So model deals with all constraints set on international (European Union), national (national culture and legislation), Insurance Organizational (ownership) and HRM level (trade union involvement and consultative arrangements). Constraints are also described as "outer" (legalistic framework, vocational training programs, social security provisions and the ownership patterns) and "internal" (union influence and employee involvement in decision making). Further, the European model shows an interaction between HR strategies, business strategy and HRM practice, and their interaction with an external environment constituting national culture, power system, legislation, education and employee representation. This means that HR strategies are closely related to the Insurance Organization strategy and external environment.

An integrative model of HRM

Considering all previously described models of HRM Martín-Alcázar in cooperation with others authors in 2005 designed an integrative model of HRM. As each of these models focuses on a specific dimension of the system, together they offer a complete explanation of this Insurance Organizational function that, in general terms, represents our common present understanding of the complex phenomenon of strategic HRM.

In model depicted in Figure 2 they define HRM as the integrated set of practices, policies and strategies through which Insurance Organizations manage their human capital that influences and is influenced by the business strategy, the Insurance Organizational context and the socio-economic context.

Both the model and this definition highlight the main dimensions of HRM: (1) horizontally, HRM is presented as the set of strategy, policies and practices that define this system relate to each other in a synergic way to manage and develop the stock of knowledge, skills and abilities of the Insurance Organization. In this sense, human capital is considered the object of HRM. Finally, the effects of the system are considered to the consequences of HRM decisions on the individual, social and Insurance Organizational level. (2) Vertically: in addition to the classical explanation of the business strategy as a contingency variable, the model considers a contextual framework for HRM characterized by a certain set of Insurance Organizational and socioeconomic variables. The bidirectional sense of these relationships lets the model explain the dynamic nature of HRM (Martín-Alcázar et al. 2005).

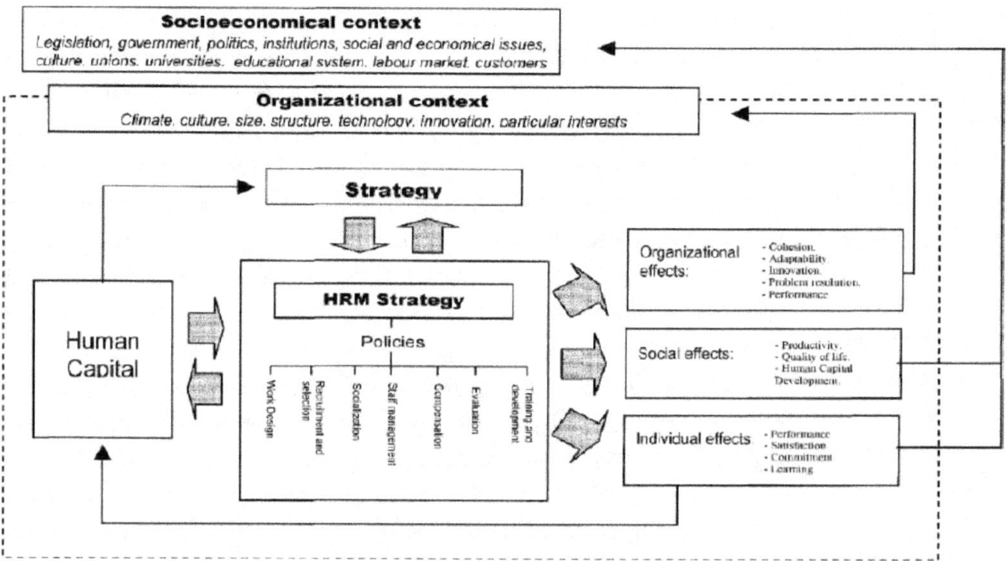

Figure 2: An integrative model for strategic human resources management

HRM process at university

This previously described integrative model was our outset to examine HRM implementation at our universities. Unfortunately, our findings were inconsiderable hence there is no significant movements in that way.

University of Zagreb has established Office for Human Relations with advisor and expert for human resource activities but there is still no any HRM strategy for whole university or any polices and guidelines. Therefore, it is up to every faculty how it will solve this problem if it even realizes that it should be solved.

For example, Faculty of Insurance Organization and Informatics University of Zagreb does not have (trained) person charged for HRM activities so decisions about workforce governance, work Insurance Organization, recruitment, education and training, career development, reward systems and other HRM activities makes Management of Faculty. Decisions are made according to arising situations so there are some procedures and systems as their result (web-based system for teaching evidence, internal webpage listing current employee status/title, emerging e-portfolio).

University of Zilina specifies following goals in the Long term aim:

To accomplish 40% share of professors and associated professors in the pedagogical and research staff.

To improve the conditions for young people (participation in the projects, social support etc.).

To support administrative staff its personal development in the frame of the Life Long Learning.

To monitor and evaluate staff numbers and its structure in order to rationalize all activities and processes. An external Insurance Organization can be engaged for this purpose.

To improve the economy and personalistic information systems in other to simplify the administration procedures and ensure an access to the dates for managers.

In present provide personnel departments only the parts of services connected with HRM. For example recruitment, personal documents´ evidence and activities connected with reward administration. The Managements of Faculties work with additional activities of HRM about career development, work Insurance Organization, workforce governance, etc. without any system approach.

Even if the strategic aims are formulated correctly at the University, it is necessary to solve the tactic part before the realization.

Indicators

In this part, with help of Budhwar's research of applicability of HRM models in India's enterprises, we list indicators of HRM models application in universities that should be examined.

The matching model

Are HRM practices and university strategy tightly connected? Does University Management believe they should develop HRM systems only for the effective implementation of their university strategies?

Does university consider their human resources (only) as a cost? Or do they invest resources to the training of them?

Are HRM strategies different for some levels of employees?

Indicators:

academic personnel involved in formation of university strategies (education, research…)

existence of HRM bodies (office, managers)

existence of HRM strategy

HRM representatives in University Management

HRM actively involved in implementation of university strategies

existence of HR development

the amount of money spent on education and training of academic employees

the amount of money spent on education and training per employee

employees trained in the areas of performance evaluation, communication, delegation, motivation, mentoring, team building

different approach to the management of professors, assistants, technical, non-technical and other employees

sharing of Insurance Organizational information with different levels of employees

5-P model

In what extent is HRM integrated into the university strategies?

What is the level of responsibility for HRM devolved to particular faculty/department/employee?

Indicators:

the translation of HRM strategy into a clear set of work programs

the responsibility of all professors, assistants, technical and non-technical personnel for implementing HRM policies

The Harvard model

How different stakeholders and situational and contingent variables influence on HRM policies and practices?

Indicators:

communication with employees through unions /work councils / suggestion box(es) / attitude survey / quality circles / web portals / e-mail and instant messages / no formal methods

recruitment through recruitment agencies / from current employees / by advertising internally / by advertising externally / by word of mouth/through apprenticeship / by use of search and selection consultants

compensation on the basis of total work experience (length of service) / participation of personnel in international and domestic projects / publishing new scientific papers or books or other online/printed material / achieving good results in work with students/other employees / work experience, performance and skills

training and development through assessment centres / annual career development interview / performance appraisal of employees / formal career plans / personal career plan / succession plans

Human Resource Management in Developing Countries

The majority of HRM studies have been conducted in the developed countries and there are still limited studies in this field in the context of developing countries (Yeganeh & Su, 2008). Budhwar and Debrah (2013) have carried out a specialized research and review on HRM in thirteen developing countries including China, South Korea, Taiwan, India, Nepal, Pakistan, Iran, Saudi Arabia, Algeria, Nigeria, Ghana, Kenya, and South Africa; this study, however, has hitherto remained among the few comprehensive explorations of the matter and, as discussed, lacks sufficient contextual and cultural understanding of the settings particularly in the case of Iran.

The term developing countries refers to the societies experiencing the process of industrialization and setting stage for economic development (Budhwar & Debrah, 2013; Napier, 1998). Some scholars believe in similarities and common denominators in terms of management styles and cultural features amongst the developing countries (Azolukwam & Perkins, 2009). Haque (1997), for instance and among others, believes that the culture of developing countries, by and large, is associated with certain values such as ethnicity, informal interaction, kinship and seniority-based authority. In this line, some

Insurance Organizational theorists distinguish between particularistic and universalistic Insurance Organizations.

Reviewing management dynamics in developing countries indicates that HRM practices in the developing societies have several characteristics in common (Budhwar & Debrah, 2004; Budhwar & Mellahi, 2006). With regard to recruitment and promotion, unlike meritocracies, certain criteria such as race, social class, language, belief system, ethnicity, gender, and loyalty to particular parties (and a mix thereof) are often given more emphasis (Haque, 1997). For example, in Bangladesh and Philippines, public Insurance

Organizations are said to be staffed with employees having strong family ties. Hence, kinship is the most important agent of recruitment and promotion (Brennan et al., 2008).

In the same vein, in Saudi Arabia and Egypt, expert power tends to be a less important criterion for selection and promotion of employees (Al-Mizjaji, 2001; Utaybi, 1992). The lack of clear criteria for appointment and promotion in Saudi Arabia, leads to some serious problems. As a consequence, nepotism has been an integral part of HR practices in this country (Budhwar & Mellahi, 2006; Utaybi, 1992). This problem is said to be the dilemma in South Africa (Beugré & Offodile, 2001) and India as well. In those countries, favoritism and assigning relatives to the work have become common to some extent (Dwivedi et al., 1989).

In Egypt, knowledge and competency does imply limited priority for appointment and selection of employees (Al-Mizjaji, 2001). Similarly, many Insurance Organizations in Oman lack job descriptions and clear career paths. Regarding recruitment, kinship often plays a significant role (Budhwar & Mellahi, 2006). As another case, in Latin America, despite the HR systems' reformation, only few countries such as Brazil, Costa Rica, Argentina, Peru, Panama, Colombia, and Ecuador follow some features of recruiting with regard to employees' competency and the others are mostly at the mercy of other factors such as family ties (Haque, 1997).

In the case of performance appraisal, most of the developing countries are reportedly putting more emphasis on loyalty, trust and friendship as the main criteria and managers, in particular, do not abide by formal and impersonal procedures (Haque, 1997). Similarly, in some cases, performance records were not kept well and the criteria for rewarding are not communicated to the employees clearly enough. Therefore, rewarding can be based on subjective criteria rather than competency as such (Pearce et al., 2000) .Similarly, compensation systems in Saudi Arabia fails to instill employees (Al-Mizjaji, 2001) and, in India, pay increases are said to be based on seniority rather than competency (Budhwar, 2000). In the same vein, in Egypt, salaries are mostly paid with regard to subjective job evaluations rather than skills and performance per se (Leat & El-Kot, 2007).

With respect to training and development, most of the training programs are often mere imitations of western programs instead of being tailored in accordance with employees' needs (Haque, 1997). For example, in South Africa as well as Saudi Arabia, training programs are not need-based and, in many cases, public Insurance Organizations confront with insufficient budgets for training. Thus, most of the training programs are tailored and implemented for specific and limited number of higher-tier employees and managers (Al-Mizjaji, 2001; Budhwar, 2000; Ghebregiorgis & Karsten, 2007). Similarly, in India, inadequate emphasis on training and development accompanied by lack of financial resources for training programs has reportedly led to poor training systems (Budhwar, 2000).

It is reported that in the great majority of developing countries, recruiting, rewarding and promotion of employees are fundamentally influenced by the relationship with and loyalty to top managers. Thus, the necessity of designing efficient, merit-based and professional HR systems is highly called for (Namazie, 2003; Namazie & Tayeb, 2006).

Employee performance

According to Hawthorne studies, and many other research work on productivity of worker highlighted the fact that employees who are satisfied with their job will have higher job performance, and thus supreme job retention, than those who are not happy with their jobs (Landy, 1985). Moreover, it is stated that employees are more likely to turnover if they are not satisfied and hence demotivated to show good performance. Employee performance is higher in happy and satisfied workers and the management find it easy to motivate high performers to attain firm targets. (Kinicki and Kreitner, 2007). The employee could be only satisfied when they feel themselves competent to perform their jobs, which is achieved through better training programs.

Recognizing the role of training practices, enable the top executives to create better working environment that ultimately improves the motivational level as well as the performance of the workforce.

According to Leonard-Barton, (1992), an organisation that gives worth to knowledge as a source of gaining competitive edge than competitors, should build up system that ensure constant learning, and on the effective way of doing so is training. Pfeffer (1994) highlights that well-trained workforce is more capable of achieving performance targets and gaining competitive advantage in the market. Training is determined as the process of enabling employee to complete the task with greater efficiency, thus considered to be vital element of managing the human resource performance strategically (Lawler, 1993; Delaney and Huselid, 1996).

The importance of training on the employee performance, through ccelerating the learning process, is mentioned in many researches (e.g. McGill and Slocum, 1993; Ulrichet al., 1993; Nonaka and Takeuchi, 1995; DiBella et al., 1996). Employee performance, achieved through training, refers to immediate improvements in the knowledge, skills and abilities to carry out job related work, and hence achieve more employee commitment towards the Insurance Organizational goals (Huselid, 1995; Ichniowski et al., 1997). Kamoche and Mueller (1998) mentioned that training should leads to the culture of enhancing learning, to raise employee performance and ultimately higher return on investment (in training) for the firm.

" A term typical to the Human Resource field, employee performance is everything about the performance of

employees in a firm or a company or an Insurance Organization. It involves all aspects which directly or indirectly affect and relate to the work of the employees" (employee performance, website).

Employee's performance important for the company to make every effort to help low performers. Performance is classified into five elements : Planning, monitoring, developing, rating and rewarding. In the planning stage ,Planning means setting goals, developing strategies, and outlining tasks and schedules to accomplish the goals.

Monitoring is the phase in which the goals are looked at to see how well one is doing to meet them .Monitoring means continously measuring performance and providing ongoing feedback to employees and work groups on their progress toward reaching their goals. Ongoing monitoring provides the opportunity to check how well employees are meeting predetermined standards and to make changes to unrealistic or problematic standards . During the developing stage an employee is supposed to improve any poor performance that has been seen during the time frame one has been working at the company. During planning and monitoring of work, deficiencies in performance become evident and can be addressed.

The rating is to summarise the employee performance. This can be beneficial for looking at and comparing performance over time or among various employees. Insurance Organizations need to know who their best performers are at the end of the cycle is rewarding stage. This stage is designed to reward and recognise outstanding behavior such as that which is better than expected.

Measures for employee performance

Ahmad and Shahzad (2011) argued that seeming performance of an employee expresses the entire conviction of an employee in regards to the actions and input to the attainment of the organisations goals and mission. They further mentioned that practices of compensation, evaluation of performance and practices concerning promotion of and employee are the benchmark for performance of a worker. So also, Anitha (2013) stated that performance of an employee is a gauge or pointer of monetary or other result of the employee that has undeviating relationship with organisation performance and accomplishment as well. Anitha, (2013) additionally disclose that atmosphere at which employee perform task and other schedules, relationship with bosses, co-employee relationship and that of team, compensation procedure, and engagement of an employee are determining factors for performance.

Conversely, Alagarajal and Shuck (2015) disclose that employee performance can be measured by means of regular training and improvement. In addition, Thomas and Feldman, (2010) take on measures of employee performance as core job performance, that includes in-role performance, security performance, and inventiveness, trailed by citizenship performance, branded into equally targets-specific and wide-ranging Insurance Organizational citizenship. As far as this study is concerned however, dimensions for measuring employee performance provided in the study of Liao et-al (2012) were chosen. This is due to the fact that the dimensions in those studies employee performance was measured from the point of view of the Insurance Organization, the employee as well as, the job itself i.e. Insurance Organizational objective, employee objective, performance development and employee satisfaction are used as measures of employee performance which makes it more wide-ranging.

Performance of an employee hence, gives room for innovativeness among employees and general firm's performance and innovativeness, in a manner that prosperous work of accomplished, inspired and zealous human resources yield ground breaking concepts for newer goods or services and also upsurge performance quality and satisfaction of the clients (Sadikoglu & Cemal, 2010).

2-3-1 Internal Research

Iran has a critical role in the middle-east economy with the second highest gross domestic production (GDP) after Saudi Arabia and second population after Egypt. The service sector contributes to more than half of Iran's GDP (World Bank, 2015). Iranian public Insurance Organizations, state-owned or semi-state-owned, entail large-scale industries and constitute more than 80% of gross domestic production. The history of Iranian public service dates back to about a century. Despite several transitions in the Iranian public service during its history, it has not been transformed fundamentally and many Insurance Organizational manifestations are rooted in the history of state management in general. The building blocks of Iranian public service were mainly reproduced during the reign of the Qajar (more than 100 years ago) based on the dominant patterns of developed countries, such as France, with undue consideration of an adaptation to the cultural requirements of the society (Saboori, 2009).

In contrast to the western countries whereby an emphasis is put on adequate prerequisites, undue preparation of the institutional structures in Iran has led to the reproduction of traditional structures in newly fabricated public service. Moreover, in the absence of strong private and nonprofit sectors, the public sector remains to define the mainstream. In spite of several efforts made by different governments during a century to improve the structure of Iranian public sector, the classic shortcomings are still apparent; these are mainly inclusive of, but not limited to, surplus labor, politicized structures, discourse of power, and low levels of efficiency, effectiveness and productivity.

As discussed, while HRM in Iran has been the subject of research in the past and scrutinized by some authors (Namazie & Frame, 2007; Namazie & Tayeb, 2006; Tayeb, 2001; Yeganeh, 2007; Yeganeh & Su, 2008), the main limitation, however, still remains to be that most of these studies are by far carried out by the authors who are living outside of

Iran. Thus, an exploration from *within* the context is promising to enhance our understanding of the subject matter. This paper aims to contribute to this gap by exploring HRM from within the context of Iran.

According to previous studies, Iranian managers typically tend to prioritize and employ their relatives and personal associates (Yeganeh & Su, 2008). In this sense, subjective judgments play a more colorful role than merit-based systems in the selection, promotion and appraisal decisions (Namazie & Frame, 2007; Yeganeh & Su, 2008).

Additionally, the relationship between pay and performance is not transparent and adequately substantiated (Yeganeh & Su, 2008); training programs are not tailored properly, and in the process of planning for HR systems, the viewpoints of employees remain by large unheard (Yeganeh, 2007).

2-3-2 Foreign Research

Lanschinger et al (2001) have suggested the role conflict, the leadership in health workers, the relationship with the supervisors, the autonomy and stress, as variables correlated with job satisfaction. Mayo (1945) had already noted group interaction as determinant of job satisfaction and highlighted the meaning of capable leadership and the achievement of satisfaction through interpersonal relations (Tovey & Adams 1999). This exact research also revealed that the behavior of the leaders affects the job satisfaction of the employees. Moreover, except from the individual factors, there are also factors in Insurance Organization level, such as Insurance Organizational culture, that affect job satisfaction. This result is consistent with the research of Gifford et al (2002), which suggests that the hospital managers should achieve a proper Insurance Organizational infrastructure, in order to augment the job satisfaction of their employees.

According to Nancarrow (2007), the decisions in a health Insurance Organization about the healthcare provided, are taken usually by a group of persons. To maintain better communication and coordination, as well as, to avoid potential conflicts, the role of leaders is important in the team motivation, in order to achieve its Insurance Organizational objective. It is found that the encouragement and support by the leaders, the confidence they inspire and their accurate vision, their consistent behavior and their ability to persuade their subordinates in recognizing their vision, are elements that can affect the job satisfaction of the employees. Additionally, Tsai (2011) in his research found that the factors that contribute to job satisfaction are not limited to the working environment of the Insurance Organization, but also include the interactions between the colleagues. The high quality in the delivery of health services requires efficient team working, it is suggested that managers of hospitals not only to create relationships within the teams providing health services, but also strive to improve these relationships in order to increase job satisfaction.

Researchers believe that Insurance Organizational culture is a complex field. It affects in different way the attitude and behavior of every employee (Van Der Post et al 1997). For example, Jacobs and Roodt (2008), revealed a correlation between the objectives of the working circle of the employees, the sharing of knowledge, the Insurance Organizational commitment, the Insurance Organizational behavior, the job satisfaction and the Insurance Organizational culture. Other academics found that Insurance Organizational culture is related to the efficiency of the Insurance Organization or its employees. According to Kane-Urrabazo (2006), a satisfying working environment can be created by the employees when the Insurance Organization promotes a sound culture and thereby it has a positive attitude towards the work of the employees. Thus, the relationship between Insurance Organizational culture and the behavior / attitude of the employee has been proved by various scholars, in several fields (Tsui et al 2006). Finally, Jacobs and Roodt (2008), noted a positive correlation between Insurance Organizational culture and job satisfaction of the employees.

Regarding health Insurance Organizations of Greek state, the research had been scarce, in relation to their Insurance Organizational culture or to the job satisfaction of their workforce. Even less is the academic association of Insurance Organizational culture with the job satisfaction of the employees of health institutions in Greece.

Polyzos and Ifantopoulos (2000), in a study carried out on the development of human resources in 113 Greek health Insurance Organizations, concluded that in the Insurance Organizational and administrative level, there is no clear separation of responsibilities inside the departments and of the range of responsibility and duties of the executives.

Sakellaropoulos (2006), in a survey conducted on the nursing staff of the two largest hospitals of Patras, observed in relation the job satisfaction of the workers, moderate emotional exhaustion in general, high exhaustion by the lack of personal achievements and high depersonalization. Augmented levels of emotional exhaustion were observed at higher educated employees. Similarly, job satisfaction was found to be low, corresponding to moderate dissatisfaction from work. It appeared the decreased job satisfaction to be associated with the older age, poor working environment and the higher experience level. Also, it was observed a negative correlation between emotional exhaustion and job satisfaction.

In the Greek literature, there are recorded three surveys conducted based on the questionnaire of the Model of Competitive Values – OCAI of Quinn and Cameron (1999). These are the doctoral thesis of Pardalis (2005), the journal article of Chondrokouki and Papageorgiou (2010) and the thesis of Kntzoura (2011). The first on took place in four public hospitals of Greece, which were selected according to their geographical position. The second survey included twelve Greek public hospitals and the third was held in the University Hospital of Pulmonary Diseases "SOTIRIA". All of these surveys had as framework the medical, nursing, administrative and technical personnel of the hospitals under survey.

With regard to the results of the responses, it is obvious by the comparison of the four formentioned surveys slight differences. Especially, the opinions of the employees as they derived from the first two surveys, rank the Hierarchy type of culture as the dominant type of culture inside the Insurance Organizations, coming to accordance with the present research. It is proved that the Greek public hospitals are characterized by introversion, formalistic compliance with the rules, focusing on bureaucracy and hierarchical structures, while maintaining stability. The results do not differ either in how the employees want the culture of the Insurance Organization to be shaped in the next five years. Also in this case emerges as dominant culture of the health Insurance Organization the Hierarchical type of culture. Certainly, the degree of intensity of this type of culture is smaller and a common desire of the majority of the employees is expressed, for a more balanced culture in the future, which will be based on all the four types of culture.

According to Kastanioti et al (2011), in their survey made in the public hospitals of Peloponnese, the Insurance Organizational culture is an important variable in the management of health units. So, according to the perceptions of the hospital managers, job characteristics that seem to emerge as important is the attention, the respect of human rights, the fairness, the accuracy, the individual responsibility, the effective organizing, the emphasis on quality, the orientation to people, the flexibility and the attention to details, while less important are highlighted the long working hours and the promotion of aggressive behavior. On the other hand, the health Insurance Organization, according to the perceptions of its employees, seems to give emphasis on features that are not found in high levels in the expectations of the individuals. In particulars, it promotes the adaptability, the predictability and the willingness to work long hours. It seems that the age, the position and the working experience of the employees affects their perceptions about the dimensions of Insurance Organizational culture, opposed to the gender and the specialty. The authors concluded, therefore, that public hospitals of Peloponnese do not seem to be governed by a strong culture. According to the perceptions of the executives, there is a gap between the ideal and the existing Insurance Organizational culture.

Finally, Tsiamanta (2012), studying the General Hospital of Volos, concluded that determination of the Insurance Organizational culture of the hospital, can provide important information about the existing culture of the Insurance Organization, both at an overall level and team level according to specific criteria. If the management of the health Insurance Organization can exploit the data obtained, can be led to the development and implementation of solutions that lead to a more efficient and effective administration, which will help to create competitive advantage. These changes can make the hospital dominant in an area, magnetizing more users of its services. In conclusion, the knowledge of the culture of an Insurance Organization can act as an effective weapon against a fast pace changing environment. The information drawn from this knowledge can be in vast amount and is likely to offer solutions to the problems of the health Insurance Organization. This may be the beginning of a constructive change, aiming to improve the quality and efficiency of health services (Kastanioti et al 2011).

2-4 Research designing conceptual model

Denison (1984) studied 34 Americans cultural performance on basis of characteristics that helps in improving Human Resource Productivity over time. The culture and Human Resource Productivity have been interrelated to each other based upon perfect association between business processes. The culture construct based upon operational complexity have its basis towards different business processes. In more than 200 Insurance Organizations economic and long term performance have been investigated (Kotter and Heskett ,1992). Several researches have been made to evaluate Human Resource Productivity of Insurance Organization based upon efforts as culture has been given significant association.

Research Framework Research hypothesis has been tested based by two theories that are Robbins and ACHIEVE theory. Robbins theory is used to investigate the factors effect on Insurance Organizational culture, which includes 10 indicators: corporate identity, risk-taking, goal clarity, Insurance Organizational integration, support management, control, individual creativity, reward systems, conflict-taking, corporate communications. ACHIEVE theory is used to assess the Factors that effect on staff productivity. This theory includes 7 indicators that are Ability, Clarity, Help, Incentive, Evaluation, Validity and Environment.

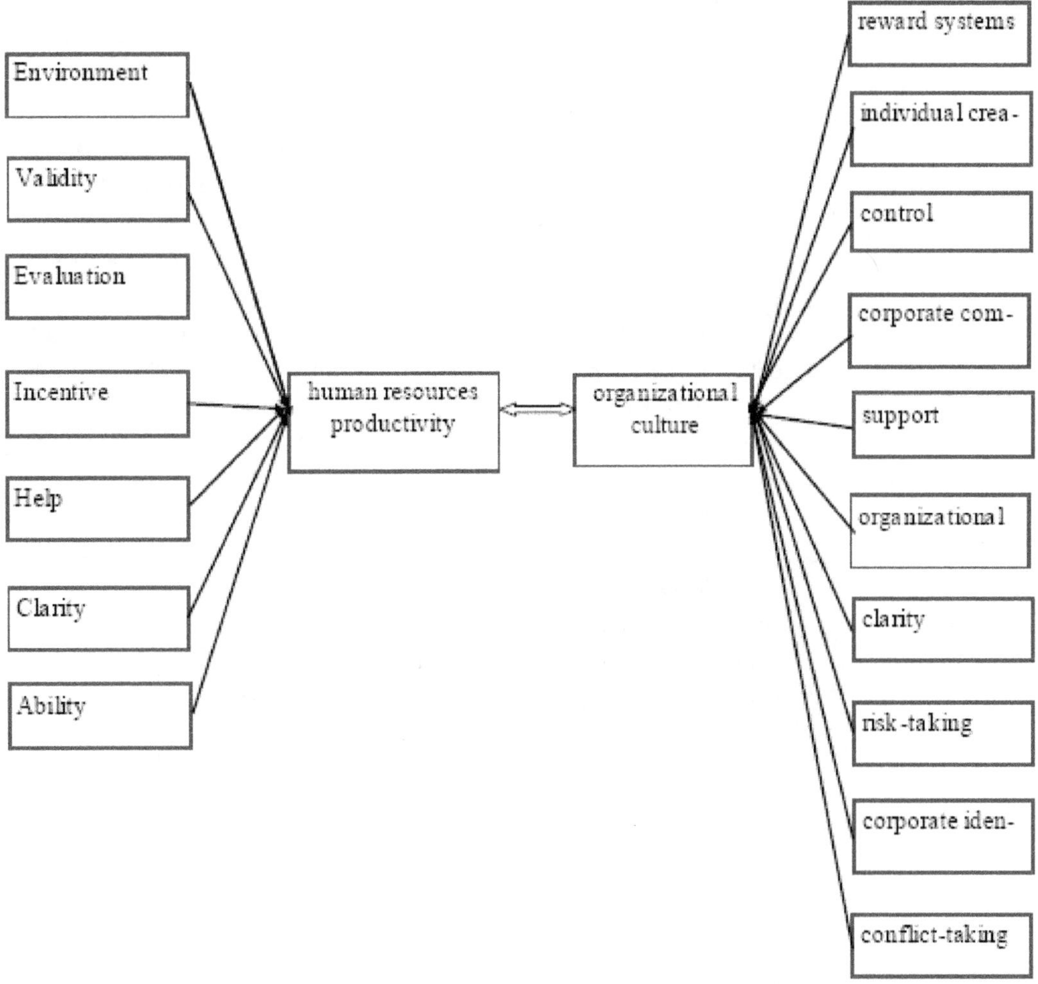

Summary

Almost all Insurance Organizations develop a dominant type of Insurance Organizational culture over time, and these culture types can be reliably and validly assessed using an instrument based on the Competing Values Framework (see Cameron & Quinn, 1999). Particular types of cultures form as certain values, assumptions, and priorities become dominant when Insurance Organization address challenges and adjust to changes. These dominant cultures help the Insurance Organization remain consistent and stable as well as adaptable and flexible in dealing with a rapidly changing environment. Whereas Insurance Organizational cultures often evolve in predictable ways over time (Cameron & Whetten, 1981;Quinn & Cameron, 1983) Insurance Organizations face the need to change cultures as a result of environmental jolts, mergers and acquisitions, new marketplace opportunities, or the need to implement certain kinds of strategic or structural changes. Without a change in culture, for example, most change initiatives such as TQM, downsizing, mergers and acquisitions, and teamwork often fall short of expectations (Cameron, 1997). The problem with trying to change Insurance Organizational culture is that it is so amorphous and vague. It is hard to know what to target and where to begin. Culture is often the catch-all concept for almost anything in Insurance Organizations that is difficult to specify or assess. This article has explained one relatively well-accepted process for effectively leading Insurance Organizational culture change. An instrument has been discussed that helps assess the Insurance Organization's current culture, its preferred future culture, and the strategic leadership activities that are needed to help culture change occur.

The main objectives in outlining this assessment process, including the seven steps for implementing culture change, are to help ensure that the Insurance Organization is clear from the outset regarding what its current culture is and why it needs to change. A common mistake in Insurance Organizations desiring to improve is that they do not create a common viewpoint regarding where the Insurance Organization is starting and how that differs from an ideal future state. Unsuccessful Insurance Organizations often launch a change initiative without considering the need to develop a consensual view of the current culture; to reach consensus on what change means and doesn't mean; the specific changes that will be started, stopped, and enhanced; the small wins and celebrations that are required; the measures, metrics, and milestones required for accountability; the requisite communication system needed; and the on-going leadership demands faced by Insurance Organizations in the midst of culture change (Cameron, 1997). This explanation provides a short but well-tested formula for overcoming the common obstacles to culture change and helping to make the process of culture change more systematic.

2-5 Chapter Summary

In this chapter, we became acquainted with the definitions of independent and dependent variables, and we reviewed the literature and past history and the variables of the subject that we found. Variables in general and in part in other researches, what effect do they have on other positions or what results they bring in the next stage. By mapping conceptual model and full definitions and society, their variables and dimensions were discussed.

Chapter III

Research Methodology

3-1-Introduction

In this chapter, the methodology used in this research has been introduced and the statistical society and the statistical sample and how they will be chosen will be examined. Subsequently, the data collection method and the variables studied are discussed. After determining the sample size, the type of research method that is appropriate to the goals and subject of the research was selected. The research method of this research is applied and correlation type and finally, the statistical techniques are used.

Methodology is the mean of knowing each science. Methodology in its absolute sense is called the methods used to reach scientific knowledge, and the methodology of each science is also the appropriate and accepted method of that science for understanding its norms and rules. Methods of recognition should be distinguished from the methods of their implementation techniques. Because the implementation of each rule after it is understood is possible.

It will also discuss the choice of the research period and its domains, the statistical population, and the sample of the research, data collection methods, and other issues related to the methodology of the research.

3.2 Research Subject

The choice of the topic of research is the first step in the formulation and implementation of a research project. It should be noted that selecting an appropriate subject in research in a discipline of science requires familiarization with the principles, rules, and scientific theories that make up the field and identify its latest developments. Accordingly, in choosing the subject of research, attention should be paid to issues such as researcher's interest, excitement, researcher, importance and priority, researcher's ability, material resources, information resources, time constraints, and the importance of research (Sarmad et al., 2009) According to the above, the subject of this research is " **Insurance Organization's Culture can impact Human Resource Productivity** ".

3. 3. Research Methodology

The present research is descriptive in terms of implementation method. Descriptive research involves collecting information to test the hypothesis or answer questions related to the current state of the subject. A typical example of descriptive research is the evaluation of attitudes or beliefs towards individuals, Insurance Organizations, events or practices. The descriptive research describes and interprets what it is and relates to existing situations, existing beliefs, current processes, evident effects, or trends in expanding attention. Attention is primarily given to it, although it often examines past events and effects that are relevant to existing conditions. (Khaki, 2005: 92). In this method, there is no experimental manipulation in the variables and its purpose is to describe social realities from the point of view of individuals, not from the viewer's point of view. (Delavar, 2005: 141)

3-4-Algorithm of the Research Method

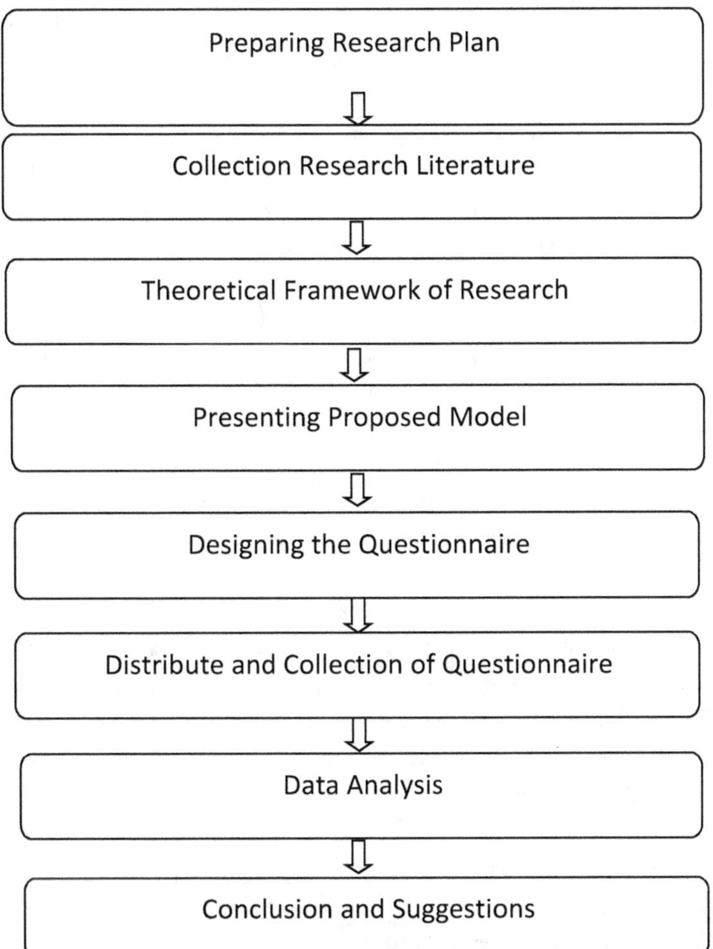

3-4 Statistical Population:

The main purpose of the research is to discover the truths that are true in most cases, and this discovery of the truth is done by collecting data from examples of the statistical community. A community is a statistical society that the researcher wants to study about the variable's characteristics of its units. The sample is a smaller group of people selected for viewing and analysis. In fact, the selected samples must be representative of the community. A community is a group of individuals, objects, or events that have at least one commonality or attribute. In the research, the concept of society refers to all individuals whose generalizability is practiced. Society in fact includes all the elements that matter in a given research, and we want to infer it. (Hooman, 2005: 115). The surveyed society in this research is a total number of employees of SAMAN insurance company that is considered as a statistical sample.

3-5. Information Gathering Method

In order to collect theoretical foundations of information about explanation of the literature, the subject of the research was used by library method and documentary studies. One of the main methods for collecting data in this research is the library method. So that the theoretical topics needed for research were collected from related resources including books, articles, theses, as well as resources in databases and libraries of universities and higher education institutions.

Data can be collected through observation, interviewing, content analysis, questionnaires or other techniques. However, the questionnaire is the most common technique used in the survey, but there is not necessarily a link between survey research and the questionnaire. The questionnaire is a very technical tool for data collection in which each questioner is asked for the same set of questions. For this reason, the questionnaire provides a highly efficient method for the formation of a variable matrix, as the case may be, for large instances. The creation of a questionnaire has four aspects: the choice of territories and the questions we are asking about, making real questions, evaluating questions, and designing a suitable questionnaire. (Hooman, 2005: 85)

In the forthcoming research, the mentioned cases are considered in the formulation of the questionnaire. It should be noted that in this research, a theoretical part of the documentary method is used and the survey method is used in the field of measurement and analysis. The data gathering tool is a questionnaire which is carried out by referring to the sample and completing the questionnaire by the researcher. In general, the method of collecting information is through the documentary method and the questionnaire.

3-5-1. The Structure of the Research Questionnaire

A questionnaire is one of the common tools for research and is a direct method for obtaining research data. The questionnaire is a set of questions that they provide with the necessary answers. This answer is the data needed by the researcher. Questionnaires are a kind of stimulus-response. Questionnaires can be used to assess the knowledge, interests, attitudes and beliefs of a person and understanding previous experiences and getting to know what's going on right now.

In order to meet the research objectives, respondents' views are collected through a questionnaire. The questionnaire consists of the following two parts:

Part One: Demographic information of respondents, including gender, age, work record, and educational level.

Part Two: The main questions are based on library studies.

3-5-2. The Process of Setting Up the Questionnaire and Results of the Preliminary Study and Pre-Test

In order to measure the characteristics of the study, based on the research objectives, the existing records of the research have been selected and based on the judicative validity of the indicators for the selection in the questionnaire. Before performing the final sampling, the reliability of the questionnaire, the method of work and probable implementation problems were checked to ensure the validity of the questionnaire, a preliminary study on a small random sample of 30 subjects from the statistical population. At this stage, a face validity is examined using the sample members' view of the degree of clarity of questions or ambiguity. In this stage, the reliability of the questionnaire is examined by Cronbach's alpha coefficient. Cronbach's alpha coefficient and correlation coefficient were used to check the reliability of the questionnaire. Therefore, if the validity and reliability of the final questionnaire were approved in the preliminary study and pre-test phase, then in the next step it will be prepared for the final sample on the research.

3-6. Validity and Reliability

No measure is immune of the error, but the measurement issue includes a degree of error that is called a measurement error. It is not possible to avoid full error, but our goal is to reduce the measurement error as much as possible. The most important criterion for measuring accuracy is validity and reliability, that is, does a researcher really measure what he thinks? Is it possible to generalize data and findings? There are various tests for checking the reliability. In this study, internal and external validity tests have been used.

External or external credentials, i.e., whether the results of the research can be extended to a larger group or similar groups of research (Sarai, 2010). To obtain this result, random sampling should be used. This means that if our selected sample is selected in randomized research (that is, there is equal chance for all members of the statistical society), it is assumed that the characteristics of the statistical society will be gained proportionally. Therefore, the findings of the research can be generalized to the relevant statistical community and acknowledged that the work has external validity. Regarding the fact that the present research is carried out using sampling methods, it can be said that the results of the sample in this study can be generalized to the whole society.

Internal or content validity, i.e., a careful examination of the concept of meaning and the question of whether the instrument of measurement really measures the concept. (Hooman, 2011). In this research, the criteria used in this study to ensure content validity of the questionnaire are:

1. Conducting theoretical studies. 2. Discussion of supervisors and professors (5 people), consultants and other experts (10 people). 3. Using the previously tested questions. Finally, the questionnaire's mistakes are inadequate and obscure. Some items and ... will be resolved.

In addition to validity, the measurement must have stable and reliable. Reliability is one of the characteristics of a measuring instrument and it deals with the extent to which the measurement tool under the same conditions yields the same results. (Sarmad et al., 2011). In other words, in order to assess or scientific trust, it is necessary to obtain similar results in the repetition of previous acts. (Saroukhani, 2011)

One of the most common methods for measuring the reliability of questionnaires is the Cronbach's alpha test, which is used to determine the internal consistency of the measurement scale. The Cronbach Alpha value is between zero and one ($0 < \alpha < 1$). If $\alpha = 1$, the indication of the accuracy of the measuring instrument and vice versa of $\alpha = 0$ indicates the inaccuracy and repeatability of the measurement. Cronbach's alpha coefficients equal to or greater than $\propto = 0/5$ represent the appropriate reliability of the measuring instrument. This test applies to questions that measure a whole concept in a general way. Therefore, it is very appropriate to measure the reliability of the results of the Likert scale. As it is known, the reliability test is done to remove the inappropriate items. Therefore, in order to eliminate inappropriate items, the reliability of the items and the variables of the research are examined. Also, for reliability measure in this study, Cronbach's alpha is used.

3-6-1. Reliability of the Questionnaire

Reliability of the scale of the questionnaire was done by pre-test of 30 questionnaires distributed and performed as follows is presented in Table 3-6. The Cronbach Alpha values obtained for the sub-indices are acceptable, and therefore the reliability of the questionnaire is confirmed, because all the components are above 0.70. And the overall point in the questionnaire section is 0.897, which indicates good reliability.

Table 3-5, Cronbach's Alpha Coefficient

Cronbach Alpha	Scale
0.896	Questionnaire
0.905	Human Resource Productivity
0.882	Insurance Organization's Culture

3-7. Variables and Research Model

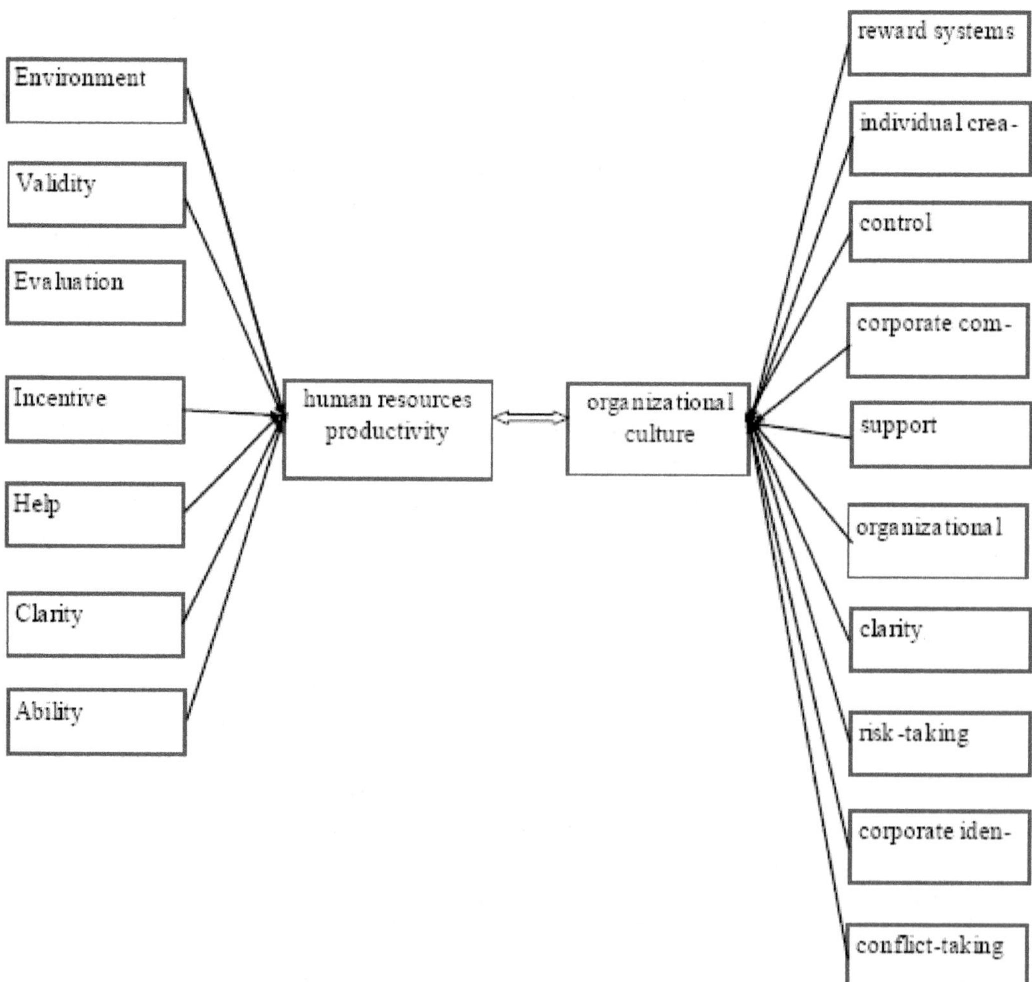

3-7. Data Analysis Method

In general, analysis is the method in which the entire research process is directed towards a result. For this purpose, descriptive and inferential statistics techniques have been used. Descriptive statistics have been used to categorize the responses of the questionnaire and to convert them to the research variables and to use descriptive statistics techniques such as creating frequency tables and plotting statistical charts to examine the distribution. The statistical sample is considered in terms of variables such as age, gender, work record, and occupational status. Inferential statistics is the part of statistics that relies on estimating the hypothesis test on the parameters of society from the sample. The inference from the sample cannot be conclusive, and these inferences are probable, and therefore the basis of probability theory in their expression is in fact, the ultimate goal of inferential statistics is to identify the characteristics of the society. To analyze the research data and the statistical deduction, various analyzes have been used. In this research, SPSS software is used to analyze the data. According to the proposed model and the research variables that are related to each other, we use the spss software to determine the internal and external relationships of the variables. Using this software, correlation and the relationship of variables were analyzed using parametric or nonparametric tests.

3-8. Summary of the Chapter

In this chapter, firstly, based on the theoretical foundations of the research, the spatial, temporal and community domains, and the statistical sample of the research was expressed. The following chapter discusses how to collect the information needed for research, and at the end of the chapter, the test method was expressed by the variables of the research. In the fourth chapter, we report the results of the hypothesis test and analyze their findings.

Chapter IV

4.1 Introduction

The collected data is raw data, and statistics are used to measure them in order to realize the goals of research and research. The analysis of information as part of the scientific research methodology is one of the main pillars of each study and research, through which all research activities are managed to achieve a result. In other words, in this section, the researcher uses a variety of analytical methods to answer the question, or decides whether to reject or confirm the hypothesis or assumptions that are considered for the research. Therefore, it is necessary to note that the analysis of the data obtained alone is not enough to find the answer to the research questions, interpreting these data is also necessary. First, we must analyze the data and then interpret the results of this analysis. Data were collected from a questionnaire whose validity was tested. This information was analyzed in SPSS software using appropriate statistical tests according to the research hypotheses. In this chapter, the results were collected and the data analysis was performed on the basis of statistical inference and appropriate statistical techniques in order to confirm or rejecting the research hypothesis.

In this section, in order to describe the characteristics of the sample, the collected data are first summarized and classified using descriptive statistics indices, after which descriptive statistics including the mean, standard deviation of the given variables were given, then using the inferential statistics indexes to confirm or reject assumptions.

4-1-1 Data

A set of numbers, letters, and signs that are logged into a computer on a contractual basis and are worthless without processing. An example of data can be referred to as zero and one memory, which is worthless without processing. The data includes facts and forms that are meaningless for the user. When these data are processed, they become information.

Information is processed data, or meaningful data. Data conversion is done by a data processor. Information processor is one of the key elements of the perceptual system. The processor of information can include computer elements, non-linear elements, or a combination of the two. (Mcleod, pp. 16-15: 1998)

4-1-2- Information Supply Sources

Information in human-machine complex systems is fed from the following resources:

- Availability of management environment information
- Information storage methods for operating system operating systems
- Information transfer methods
- How to connect
- Storage and retrieval

The first major application of the computer was the processing of accounting data. The application was accompanied by four other operations: management information systems, decision support systems, virtual administration, and knowledge-based systems; all of these five applications comprise a computerized information system

After processing on the data, the result of the work is the production of information. The generated information has its own value, while the value of the information depends on the amount of help it decides and improves in management behavior.

Information in each situation has specific features that these features are as follows:

Information accuracy: Information may be incorrect or incorrect if the producer of the information is wrong.

- Information Form: Information can be in various ways such as numeric, textual, and so on information.
- Frequency or Repetition: Information is usually repeated every time, such as the annual balance sheet, monthly salary
- Information relevance: Information is considered relevant when required for a particular situation.
- Complete Information: Information is complete when it satisfies all consumer needs.
- Timeliness of information: Information should be made according to time.
- Amount of information: Information may cover a large or small amount of scope. Source of information: Information can be from internal sources of the Insurance Organization or outside the Insurance Organization.
- Timeline Information: Information may be related to the present, future or past.

Source of information: The source of information can be divided into two primary and secondary categories:

A. Source: Primary Information: View

Experimental surveys

Estimates

B. secondary information source

Information that is purchased from foreign sources.

Provide information from publications, written media, organs, government agencies

3-1-4 Processing system

The subject of processing is based on two data and information axes, which can be used to describe data and information as follows:

The data are symbols and symbols that represent events that have happened. These symbols are in words and shapes, and so on.

Information is the knowledge of the recipient of the message he receives. If the message does not have such a feature, it is considered to be the recipient of the data; information may be in the form of language, behavioral symptoms, or other signs and symptoms, as well as the concept of information and relative data.

Data processing and data include recording, sorting, combining, calculating, aggregation, storing, retrieving, re-generating, and ....

4.1.4. Data analysis

Data analysis is a multi-stage process in which data collected through the use of collection tools in a statistical sample (community) are summarized, coded and categorized, ... and finally processed, so that the background Establishing various types of analysis and communication between these data in order to test the hypotheses.

In this process, both conceptual and empirical data are refined, and various statistical techniques play a significant role in deductions and generalizations. Although analytical processes vary according to the type of research, the research issue, the nature of the hypotheses, the type of the theory, the tools used to collect information, ... but have different stages.

To analyze data and information based on predefined goals, the data for each of the variables, which are the result of the questionnaire response, are described in terms of statistical numerical attributes and then, using appropriate statistical models, the research hypotheses have been tested and final analysis has been done in the final stage.

4.1.6 Statistical Community

The surveyed society in this research is a whole range of SAMAN insurance Employees that is considered as a statistical society. The number of samples is 168 for the SAMAN insurance Employees. However, to eliminate the effects of incomplete and missing questionnaires, 15% of the sample size was added. Accordingly, 193 questionnaires will be distributed among the community. Finally, 193 questionnaires will be used to analyze the statistics.

4-1-7. Distribution of the Frequency of the Age of the Subjects

In distributing the abundance of tables and charts (1-4), we review the age of our employee by examining the age of the SAMAN insurance Employees to find out what is percentage of customers' age at SAMAN insurance Employees.

Table 4-1: Age of Respondents

Frequency percentage	Frequency		
33.2	64	Less than 30 years old	
62.7	121	Between 30 to 50 years old	
4.1	8	More than 50 years old	

100.0	193	Total	

Figure 4-1: The age of the respondents

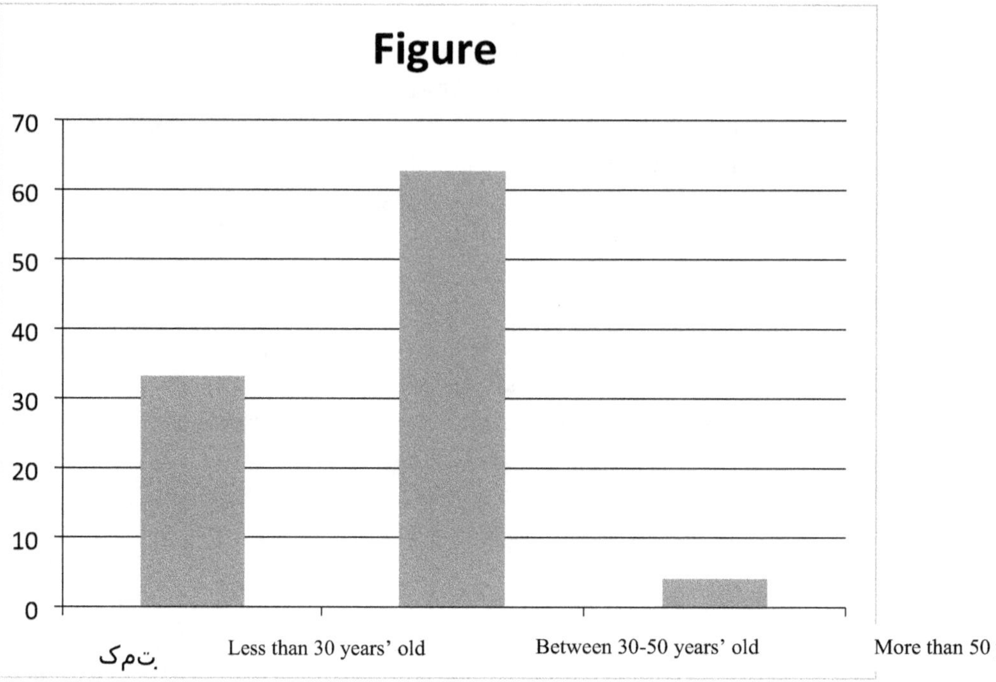

4.9. Distribution of Frequency of gender:

This part of the gender is the answer to the questionnaires of SAMAN insurance Employees.

Table 4.1: Information about the gender of the respondents

Frequency percentage	Frequency		
92.2	178	Man	
7.8	15	Female	
100.0	193	Total	

Figure 1-2: Gender of respondents

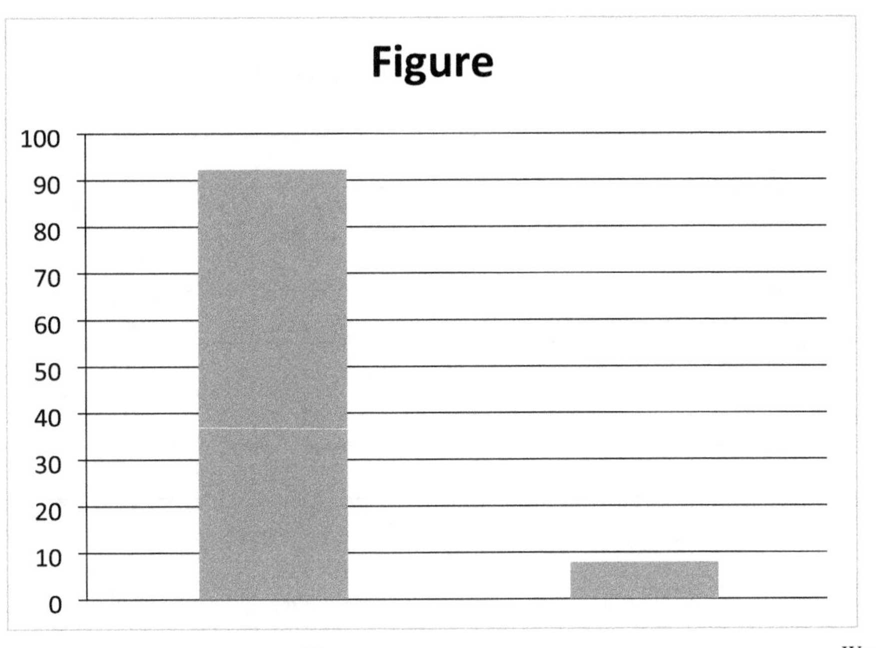

4-9. Frequency distribution of education:

This section relates to the level of education of SAMAN insurance Employees.

Table 4: Level of education of respondents

Frequency percentage	Frequency	
3.1	6	Less than diploma
3.1	6	Diploma
20.2	39	Associate Degree
72.0	139	BA
1.6	3	Master's degree and higher
100.0	193	Total

Figure 4-3: Level of Respondents Education

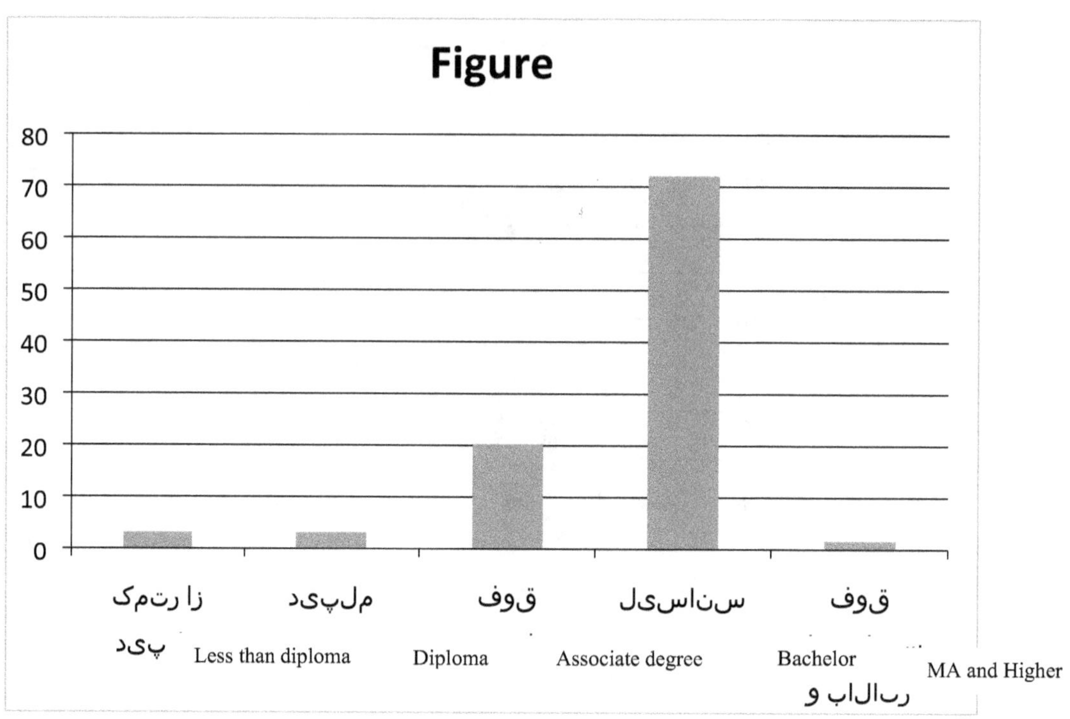

4-9. Distribution of history:

This section corresponds to the purchase history of answering the questionnaires of employee at SAMAN insurance.

Table 4-3: Executive Records of Respondents

Frequency percentage	Frequency	
28.5	55	Less than 5 years
50.8	98	Between 5 and 10 years
17.1	33	Between 10 and 20 years
3.6	7	More than 20 years
100.0	193	Total

Chart 4-4: executive records of Respondents

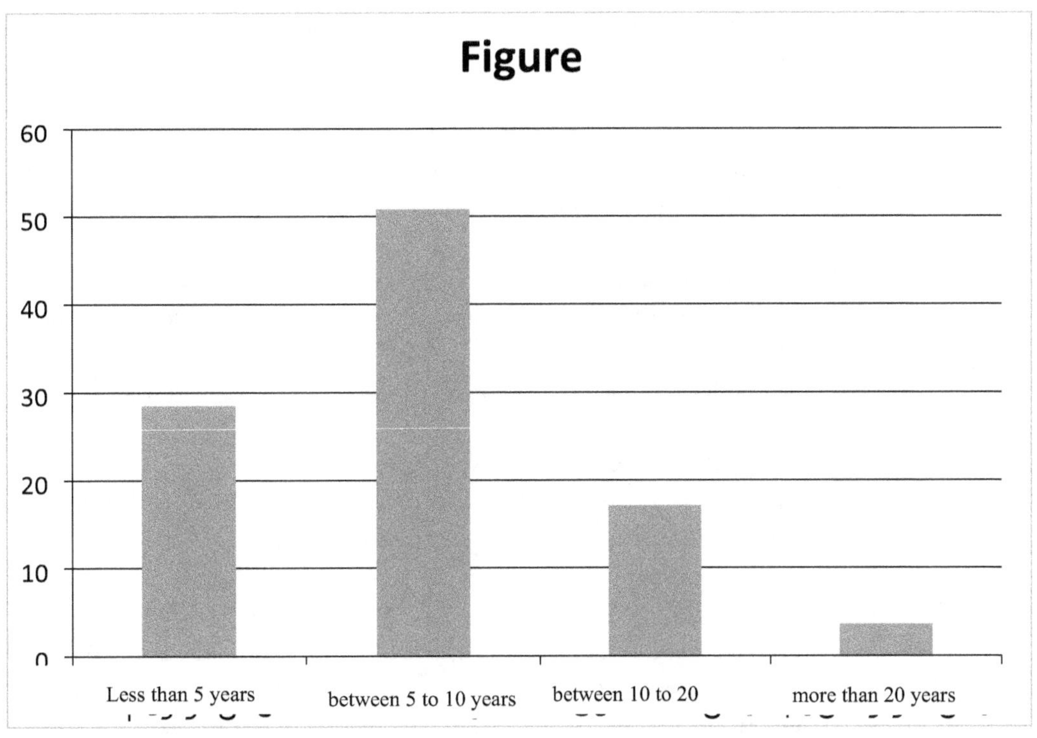

4-10 The main hypothesis

Main hypothesis:

Specificities of an Insurance Organization's Culture has effect on Human Resource Productivity

To test the research hypotheses, the T test was used. For this purpose, the mean variables were compared to the middle of the measuring instrument scale, that is, the number 3, which the results of the tests are divided into each of the variables. The statistical assumptions of the T test are as follows:

The main hypothesis

Specificities of an Insurance Organization's Culture has effect on Human Resource Productivity

. 3 H0: $\mu = 3$

Specificities of an Insurance Organization's Culture doesn't effect on Human Resource Productivity

. 3 H1: $\mu \neq 3$

Table 4.9. T-test results for the first hypothesis of the study

Error level	Freedom degree	t	Average difference	Number	Variable
0.000	199	117.58	3.984	193	Insurance Organizational culture
Error level	Freedom degree	t	Average difference	Number	Variable
0.000	199	101.58	3.124	193	Human resource productivity

Considering that the t-single sample calculated for the first hypothesis of the research according to (P=0.000), the role of Specificities of an Insurance Organization's Culture effect on Human Resource Productivity 95% is acceptable. Given that, the average Insurance Organization culture difference is 3,984 and the difference is the average human resource productivity is 101.58. As a result, Specificities of an Insurance Organization's Culture has effect on Human Resource Productivity

4-11. Sub-hypothesis

First sub-hypothesis:

Specificities of an Insurance Organization's Culture has impact on employee ability H0: $\mu = 3$

Specificities of an Insurance Organization's Culture doesn't impact on employee ability. H1: $\mu \neq 3$

Table 10.4. T-test results for the first sub-hypothesis

Error level	Freedom degree	T	Average difference	Number	Variable
0.000	199	80.31	3.49	193	Employee ability

Considering that the t-single-sample calculated for the second main hypothesis of the research according to (P=0.000), the role of Specificities of an Insurance Organization's Culture with employee ability of 95%. Considering the average difference is 3.49. As a result, Specificities of an Insurance Organization's Culture has impact on employee ability

Second sub hypothesis:

Specificities of an Insurance Organization's Culture has effect on job clarity by staff. H0: $\mu=3$

Specificities of an Insurance Organization's Culture has effect on job clarity by staff. H1: $\mu \neq 3$

Table 4-11. T-test results for the second sub-hypothesis of the study

Error level	Freedom degree	T	Average difference	Number	Variable
0.000	199	87.29	3.72	193	job clarity by staff

Considering that the t-single sample calculated for the first sub-hypothesis of the research according to (P=0.000), the role of Insurance Organizational culture with job clarity by staff of 95% is rejected. Considering that the average difference is 3.72. As a result Specificities of an Insurance Organization's Culture has effect on job clarity by staff.

Third sub hypothesis:

Specificities of an Insurance Organization's Culture has effect on Insurance Organizational help. H0: $\mu=3$

Specificities of an Insurance Organization's Culture doesn't effect on Insurance Organizational help. H1: $\mu \neq 3$

Table 12.3. T-test results for the third sub-hypothesis of the study

Error level	Freedom degree	t	Average difference	Number	Variable
0.000	199	83.65	3.83	193	Insurance Organizational help

Given that the t-single-sample calculated for the first hypothesis of the research according to (P=0.000), the role of Insurance Organizational culture with a Insurance Organizational help of 95% of the hypothesis is not acceptable. Considering the average difference is 3.83. As a result, Specificities of an Insurance Organization's Culture has effect on Insurance Organizational help.

Fourth sub-hypothesis:

Specificities of an Insurance Organization's Culture has effect on employee incentive. H0: $\mu=3$

Specificities of an Insurance Organization's Culture does not effect on employee incentive. H1: $\mu \neq 3$

Table 4-14. T-test results for the fourth sub-hypothesis of the research

Error level	Freedom degree	t	Average difference	Number	Variable
0.000	199	85.58	3.98	193	employee incentive

Considering that the t-single sample calculated for the first sub-hypothesis of the research according to (P=0.000), the role of Insurance Organizational culture with the employee incentive of 95% of the hypothesis is acceptable. Given that the difference is an average of 3.98. As a result, Specificities of an Insurance Organization's Culture has effect on employee incentive.

Fifth sub hypothesis:

Specificities of an Insurance Organization's Culture has effect on employee evaluation. H0: $\mu=3$

Specificities of an Insurance Organization's Culture doesn't effect on employee evaluation. H1: $\mu \neq 3$

Table 4-15. T-test results for the fifth sub-hypothesis of the study

Error level	Freedom degree	t	Average difference	Number	Variable
0.000	199	85.55	3.92	193	employee evaluation

Given the fact that the t-single sample calculated for the first sub-hypothesis of the study according to (P=0.000), the role of the employee evaluation with the Insurance Organizational culture of 95% is acceptable. Considering the average difference is 3.92. As a result, Specificities of an Insurance Organization's Culture has effect on employee evaluation.

Sixth sub hypothesis:

Specificities of an Insurance Organization's Culture has effect on employee validity. H0: μ=3

Specificities of an Insurance Organization's Culture doesn't effect on employee validity H1: μ≠3

Table 4-16. Results of the t test for the sixth sub-hypothesis of the study

Error level	Freedom degree	t	Average difference	Number	Variable
0.000	199	84.95	3.63	193	employee validity

Considering that the t-single sample calculated for the first sub-hypothesis of the research according to (P=0.000), the is Specificities of an Insurance Organization's Culture acceptable with employee validity of 95%. Considering the average difference is 3.63. As a result, Specificities of an Insurance Organization's Culture has effect on employee validity.

Seventh sub hypothesis:

Specificities of an Insurance Organization's Culture has effect on employees environmentally. H0: μ=3

Specificities of an Insurance Organization's Culture doesn't effect on employees environmentally. H1: μ≠3

Table 4.17. T-test results for the seventh sub-hypothesis of the research

Erro r level	Freedo m degree	t	Average differen ce	Numb er	Variable
0.00 0	199	85.3 6	3.89	193	employees environmental ly

Given that the t-single-sample calculated for the first sub-hypothesis of the research according to (P=0.000), the role of Specificities of an Insurance Organization's Culture is accepted with a employees environmentally of 95%. Considering the average difference is 3.89. As a result, Specificities of an Insurance Organization's Culture has effect on employees environmentally.

Eighth Sub-hypothesis:

Human Resource Productivity has impact on Reward systems H0: μ=3

Human Resource Productivity hasn't impact on Reward systems H1: μ≠3

Table 18.4. T-test results for the eighth sub-hypothesis of the research

Error level	Freedom degree	t	Average difference	Number	Variable
0.000	199	86.01	4.12	193	Reward systems

Considering that the t-single sample statistics calculated for the first sub-hypothesis of the research according to (P=0.000), the Reward systems is acceptable with a Human Resource Productivity of 95%. Considering the average difference is 4.12. As a result, Human Resource Productivity has impact on Reward systems.

Ninth sub hypothesis:

Human Resource Productivity has impact on Individual creativity. H0: μ=3

Human Resource Productivity has not impact on Individual creativity. H1: μ≠3

Table 4. 19- T-test results for the eighth sub-hypothesis of the research

Error level	Freedom degree	t	Average difference	Number	Variable
0.000	199	86.55	4.98	193	Individual creativity

Considering that the t-single sample calculated for the first hypothesis of the research according to (P=0.000), the role of Individual creativity with the Human Resource Productivity of 95% is acceptable. Considering the average difference is 4.98. As a result, Human Resource Productivity has impact on Individual creativity.

Tenth sub hypothesis:

Human Resource Productivity has impact on Control. H0: μ=3

Human Resource Productivity has not impact on Control. H1: μ≠3

Table 18.4. T test results for the tenth hypothesis of the research

Error level	Freedom degree	t	Average difference	Number	Variable
0.000	199	86.40	4.80	193	Control

Considering that the t-single-sample calculated for the first sub-hypothesis of the research according to (P=0.000), the role of control is acceptable with a Human Resource Productivity of 95%. Considering that the average difference is 4.80. As a result, Human Resource Productivity has impact on Control.

Elementary sub hypothesis:

Human Resource Productivity has impact on Support. H0: $\mu=3$

Human Resource Productivity hasn't impact on Support . H1: $\mu\neq3$

Table 18.4. T-test results for the eleventh hypothesis of the research

Error level	Freedom degree	t	Average difference	Number	Variable
0.000	199	86.54	4.97	193	Support

Given that the t-single sample calculated for the first hypothesis of the research according to (P=0.000), the role of support is acceptable with a Human Resource Productivity of 95%. Considering the average difference is 4.97. As a result, Human Resource Productivity has impact on Support.

The twelfth sub hypothesis:

Human Resource Productivity has impact on Clarity. H0: $\mu=3$

Human Resource Productivity hasn't impact on Clarity . H1: $\mu\neq3$

Table 4. 19- T test results for the 12th hypothesis of the research

Error level	Freedom degree	t	Average difference	Number	Variable
0.000	199	84.52	4.93	193	Clarity

Considering that the t-single sample statistics calculated for the first sub-hypothesis of research according to (P=0.000), the role of clarity with Human Resource Productivity of 95% is acceptable. Considering the average difference is 4.93. As a result of Human Resource Productivity has impact on Clarity.

Thirteenth sub-hypothesis:

Human Resource Productivity has impact on Risk taking. H0: $\mu=3$

Human Resource Productivity hasn't impact on Risk taking . H1: $\mu\neq3$

Table 10.4. T-test results for the first sub-hypothesis

Error level	Freedom degree	t	Average difference	Number	Variable
0.000	199	80.31	3.49	193	Risk taking

Considering that the t-single-sample calculated for the second main hypothesis of the research according to (P=0.000), the role of Risk taking with Human Resource

Productivity of 95%. Considering the average difference is 3.49. As a result, Human Resource Productivity has impact on Risk taking.

Fourteenth sub hypothesis:

Human Resource Productivity has impact on Corporate identification. H0: $\mu=3$

Human Resource Productivity hasn't impact on Corporate identification. H1: $\mu\neq3$

Table 4-11. T-test results for the second sub-hypothesis of the study

Error level	Freedom degree	t	Average difference	Number	Variable
0.000	199	87.29	3.72	193	Corporate identification

Considering that the t-single sample calculated for the first sub-hypothesis of the research according to (P=0.000), the role of Corporate identification with Human Resource Productivity of 95% is accepted. Considering that the average difference is 3.72. As a result Human Resource Productivity has impact on Corporate identification.

Fifteenth sub hypothesis:

Specificities of an Insurance Organization's Culture has effect on Insurance Organizational help. H0: $\mu=3$

Specificities of an Insurance Organization's Culture doesn't effect on Insurance Organizational help. H1: $\mu\neq3$

Table 12.3. T-test results for the third sub-hypothesis of the study

Error level	Freedom degree	t	Average difference	Number	Variable
0.000	199	83.65	3.83	193	Insurance Organizational help

Given that the t-single-sample calculated for the first hypothesis of the research according to (P=0.000), the role of Insurance Organizational culture with a Insurance Organizational help of 95% of the hypothesis is not acceptable. Considering the average difference is 3.83. As a result, Specificities of an Insurance Organization's Culture has effect on Insurance Organizational help.

Summary of Chapter:

This chapter analyzes the information. The collected data were raw data that was used for statistical significance. Data analysis as part of the scientific research methodology is considered as one of the main bases of each study, and this information was fully analyzed in this chapter. This information was analyzed in SPSS software using appropriate statistical tests according to the research hypotheses. In this chapter, the results are collected and the analyzed data are based on statistical inferences and appropriate statistical techniques for confirmation or rejected the research hypothesis.

Fifth Chapter: Conclusion

5.1 Introduction

Another important part of a scientific research is the discussion and conclusion and interpretation of the findings of the research. A scientific study does not end with quantitative and qualitative data analysis, and it is imperative that the extracted data be interpreted so that the necessary knowledge is extracted from the information and leads to a comprehensive understanding of the meanings and concepts of the research. Data analysis is done to answer the research questions and to identify the relationships between the phenomena proposed in the research and to interpret the rational conclusions based on the observations made in the field of research. In the present study, interpretation has been done to disclose concepts from raw data and inferential analyzes. This chapter is devoted to discussion and interpretation, in which a review of the subject was initially undertaken. Then, by re-expressing the hypotheses and presenting the result of the hypothesis, the interpretation of the results is discussed. Finally, with the mention of the research constraints, the suggestions are presented.

5.2 Research Results

Insurance Organizational culture and its environment factors in which Insurance Organization exist determines the way of managing the Insurance Organization (Saffold, 1988:547). The relationship between oInsurance Organizational culture dan human resources practices can be explained as follows. When the member of Insurance Organization i.e. employees, understand and internalized the organzationanl culture which can be said as the way things are done around here, it will enable for employee to choose strategy, and behavior that fit with their personality as well as with the main routines of Insurance Organization activities.

The main power is on the one hand, a powerful person such as the owner or the founder of the company, where "the destiny" of an employee depends on the hand of the most powerfull person (the boss). There is a division of work, the boss is the planner, the other are the doer. In the high power distance society, good leader or good manager in the eye of the employees, is someone who can act like a good father (Hofstede, 1997). This type of relationship will lead to less participative management in decision making.

The Impact of HRM on Insurance Organizational Performance

Research by Newman & Nollen (1996:753) indicated that Insurance Organization performance is better in the companies where there is congruency between national culture and human resources practice. In the unit business level, where its manager consciously practice human resource policies in accordance with country's value, the performance of business unit i.e. return on assets (ROA), return on sales is better and employee bonus is bigger.

According to Earley (1994:685) if the human resource management practices is not suitable with basic values shared by employees will cause employee are dissatisfied, uncomfortable dan uncommitted. Employee will feel distracted or alienated, because their values are diference from company expectation, and therefore, theori Insurance

Organizational commitment and their job satisfaction will be low, and in turn they may want to quit from the job. When this condition happen for a long time, Insurance Organization performance will decrease. Conversly, when human resource practice fit with the values shared by employees, Insurance Organizational performance will be high.

5-3 Conclusion of Hypotheses

Main hypothesis:

Specificities of an Insurance Organization's Culture has effect on Human Resource Productivity

To test the research hypotheses, the T test was used. For this purpose, the mean variables were compared to the middle of the measuring instrument scale, that is, the number 3, which the results of the tests are divided into each of the variables. The statistical assumptions of the T test are as follows:

Considering that the t-single sample calculated for the first hypothesis of the research according to (P=0.000), the role of Specificities of an Insurance Organization's Culture effect on Human Resource Productivity 95% is acceptable. Given that, the average Insurance Organization culture difference is 3,984 and the difference is the average human resource productivity is 101.58. As a result, Specificities of an Insurance Organization's Culture has effect on Human Resource Productivity

First sub-hypothesis:

Specificities of an Insurance Organization's Culture has impact on employee ability

Considering that the t-single-sample calculated for the second main hypothesis of the research according to (P=0.000), the role of Specificities of an Insurance Organization's Culture with employee ability of 95%. Considering the average difference is 3.49. As a result, Specificities of an Insurance Organization's Culture has impact on employee ability

Second sub hypothesis:

Specificities of an Insurance Organization's Culture has effect on job clarity by staff.

Considering that the t-single sample calculated for the first sub-hypothesis of the research according to (P=0.000), the role of Insurance Organizational culture with job clarity by staff of 95% is rejected. Considering that the average difference is 3.72. As a result Specificities of an Insurance Organization's Culture has effect on job clarity by staff.

Third sub hypothesis:

Specificities of an Insurance Organization's Culture has effect on Insurance Organizational help

Given that the t-single-sample calculated for the first hypothesis of the research according to (P=0.000), the role of Insurance Organizational culture with a Insurance Organizational help of 95% of the hypothesis is not acceptable. Considering the average difference is 3.83. As a result, Specificities of an Insurance Organization's Culture has effect on Insurance Organizational help.

Fourth sub-hypothesis:

Specificities of an Insurance Organization's Culture has effect on employee incentive.

Considering that the t-single sample calculated for the first sub-hypothesis of the research according to (P=0.000), the role of Insurance Organizational culture with the employee incentive of 95% of the hypothesis is acceptable. Given that the difference is an average of 3.98. As a result, Specificities of an Insurance Organization's Culture has effect on employee incentive.

Fifth sub hypothesis:

Specificities of an Insurance Organization's Culture has effect on employee evaluation.

Given the fact that the t-single sample calculated for the first sub-hypothesis of the study according to (P=0.000), the role of the employee evaluation with the Insurance Organizational culture of 95% is acceptable. Considering the average difference is 3.92. As a result, Specificities of an Insurance Organization's Culture has effect on employee evaluation.

Sixth sub hypothesis:

Specificities of an Insurance Organization's Culture has effect on employee validity

Considering that the t-single sample calculated for the first sub-hypothesis of the research according to (P=0.000), the is Specificities of an Insurance Organization's Culture acceptable with employee validity of 95%. Considering the average difference is 3.63. As a result, Specificities of an Insurance Organization's Culture has effect on employee validity.

Seventh sub hypothesis:

Specificities of an Insurance Organization's Culture has effect on employees environmentally.

Given that the t-single-sample calculated for the first sub-hypothesis of the research according to (P=0.000), the role of Specificities of an Insurance Organization's Culture is accepted with a employees environmentally of 95%. Considering the average difference is 3.89. As a result, Specificities of an Insurance Organization's Culture has effect on employees environmentally.

Eighth Sub-hypothesis:

Human Resource Productivity has impact on Reward systems

Considering that the t-single sample statistics calculated for the first sub-hypothesis of the research according to (P=0.000), the Reward systems is acceptable with a Human Resource Productivity of 95%. Considering the average difference is 4.12. As a result, Human Resource Productivity has impact on Reward systems.

Ninth sub hypothesis:

Human Resource Productivity has impact on Individual creativity.

Considering that the t-single sample calculated for the first hypothesis of the research according to (P=0.000), the role of Individual creativity with the Human Resource Productivity of 95% is acceptable. Considering the average difference is 4.98. As a result, Human Resource Productivity has impact on Individual creativity.

Tenth sub hypothesis:

Human Resource Productivity has impact on Control.

Considering that the t-single-sample calculated for the first sub-hypothesis of the research according to (P=0.000), the role of control is acceptable with a Human Resource Productivity of 95%. Considering that the average difference is 4.80. As a result, Human Resource Productivity has impact on Control.

Elementary sub hypothesis:

Human Resource Productivity has impact on Support

Given that the t-single sample calculated for the first hypothesis of the research according to (P=0.000), the role of support is acceptable with a Human Resource Productivity of 95%. Considering the average difference is 4.97. As a result, Human Resource Productivity has impact on Support.

The twelfth sub hypothesis:

Human Resource Productivity has impact on Clarity

Considering that the t-single sample statistics calculated for the first sub-hypothesis of research according to (P=0.000), the role of clarity with Human Resource Productivity of 95% is acceptable. Considering the average difference is 4.93. As a result of Human Resource Productivity has impact on Clarity.

Thirteenth sub-hypothesis:

Human Resource Productivity has impact on Risk taking.

Considering that the t-single-sample calculated for the second main hypothesis of the research according to (P=0.000), the role of Risk taking with Human Resource Productivity of 95%. Considering the average difference is 3.49. As a result, Human Resource Productivity has impact on Risk taking.

Fourteenth sub hypothesis:

Human Resource Productivity has impact on Corporate identification.

Considering that the t-single sample calculated for the first sub-hypothesis of the research according to (P=0.000), the role of Corporate identification with Human Resource Productivity of 95% is accepted. Considering that the average difference is 3.72. As a result Human Resource Productivity has impact on Corporate identification.

Fifteenth sub hypothesis:

Specificities of an Insurance Organization's Culture has effect on Insurance Organizational help.

Given that the t-single-sample calculated for the first hypothesis of the research according to (P=0.000), the role of Insurance Organizational culture with a Insurance Organizational help of 95% of the hypothesis is not acceptable. Considering the average difference is 3.83. As a result, Specificities of an Insurance Organization's Culture has effect on Insurance Organizational help.

5-4- Suggestions

Based on the findings of the study, the following are recommendations for the stakeholders of Insurance Organizations concerned.

(a) Create a unique culture.

Each Insurance Organization should work towards creating its own unique culture instead of copying another Insurance Organization's culture. While inspiration and ideas may be drawn from other Insurance Organizations, culture cannot be borrowed wholesale from a specific Insurance Organization. Instead, the right cultural elements must be selected, blended and fine-tuned over time to fulfill the unique requirements of one's Insurance Organization. However, although culture differs from one Insurance Organization to the other, the same culture must be shared among fellow employees within the same Insurance Organization in order to synergize and achieve common goals and vision effectively. The creation of culture need not come from the top, but it could also come from the grassroots. Therefore, Insurance Organizations must get all employees and other stakeholders involved in culture creation, whether formally or informally. An example of how this may be executed is by engaging employees in reflecting upon their company core values, work processes and best practices during team building sessions, training programs or company retreats.

(b) Link Insurance Organizational culture to HRM practice

Some leaders extol a certain culture, but yet when it comes to incentives, employees who practice the extolled culture are not recognized for their efforts, simply because the Insurance Organization's HRM function does not have a system in place. Instead, Insurance Organizations should consciously map key cultural elements to their HRM function to motivate employees to partake in the culture that the management has endorsed. This may be achieved by customizing an existing HR system in the market.

(c) Leaders must adequately mentor their staff on Insurance Organizational culture.

For Insurance Organizations that are already getting their managers or leaders to mentor subordinates, they should also ensure that the managers or leaders deal specifically with Insurance Organizational culture, and mentor their staff according to the intentions of certain cultural practices especially those that the staff find hard to comprehend or appreciate. This may be done, for example, during formal coaching or mentoring sessions, or during orientation programs for not only new employees of the Insurance Organization, but also to employees who are joining a new department

5-5 Proposal on Future Research

A Study of the Impact of Factors Affecting Specificities of an Insurance Organization's Culture

Examining the impact of factors affecting Human Resource Productivity

6.5. Research Constraints

The research respondent were HR manager/director or assistant of HR managers. They were choosen because it is assumed that they understand HRM policy and ractice in the company. However, because of their position, it is possible that their responds tend to answer the question based on their self-interest i.e. for the sake of Insurance Organizational interest, not based on what they felt as individuals. One other possible limitation was that the participants might have been able to recognize a desirable answer for the question. Besides, it relied on cross sectional and self-report data. Therefore, our ability to make causal statemet about hypothesized relationship is constrained. Longitunal studies are needed to offset the diadvantages of cross sectional design. In addition, future research, it is suggested to involve lower level employee who become the object of HRM practice, and people who are not so linked with the interest of Insurance Organization.

6-6. Summary of Chapter

In this chapter, with a general reference to the following: introduction and content of the chapter, summary of the research: summary of the three chapters, discussion: Comparison of research and results agree and opposed to the results of the findings, Conclusion: presentation of the message from the research, limitations Research: Constraints in control and beyond the control of the researcher, suggestions from the research: Proposals that can be presented with the results, suggestions to other researchers: Proposals for further research.

References

Bae, J. and Lawler, J. J. (2000). Insurance Organizational and HRM Strategies in Korea: Impact on Firm Performance in An Emerging Economy. Academy of Management Journal. Vol. 43, No.3: 502 – 517

Delaney, J.T. and Huselid, M.A. (1996). The Impact of Human Resources Management Practices on Perceptions of Insurance Organizational Performance. Academy of Management Journal, Vol.39, No.4: 949 – 969

Dessler, Gary. (1997). Manajemen Sumber Daya Manusia. Penerjemah Triyana Iskandarsyah. Penerbit PT. Prenhallindo Jakarta

Early, P. C. (1987). Intercultural Training for Managers: A Comparison of Documentary and Interpersonal Methods. Academy of Management Journal, 30, : 685 – 698

Ferdinand,A. (2002). Structural Equation Modeling dalam Penelitian Manajemen Edisi 2. Semarang: BP Undip.

Geringer, M. J., Frayne, A. C., Milliman, F. J. (2002). In Search of "Best Practices" in International Human Resource Management: Research Design and Methodology.Human Resource Management, Spring; 41, 1: 5 – 30

Hair, F.J., Anderson E.R., Tatham L.R., and Black C. W. (1998). Multivariate Data Analysis..Prentice Hall International Inc. Fifth Edition

Hofstede, G. (1980). Culture's Consequences. International Differences in Work-Related Values. A Bridged Edition. Sage Publication. Newburry Park.

Hofstede, G. (1980). Motivation, Leadership, and Insurance Organization: Do American Theories Apply Abroad? Insurance Organizational Dynamics, Summer, AMACOM, A Division of American Management Association

Hofstede, G. (1990). A Reply & Comment on Joginder P Singh: Managerial Culture and Work-related Values in India. Insurance Organization Studies, 11/1:103-106, p: 1-5

Hofstede, G. (1997). Cultures and Insurance Organizations, Software of the Mind. Intercultural Cooperation and its Importance for Survival. McGraw Hill. New York.

Jaeger, A. M. (1986). Insurance Organization Development and National Culture: Where's the Fit? Academy of Management Review. 11: 178-190

Laurent A. (1986). The Cross Cultural Puzzle of International Human Resources Management. Human Resource Management, 15: 91 – 102

Lowe, B.K, Milliman, J, De Cieri, H & Dowling, J. P. 2002. International Compensation Practices: A Ten Country Comparative Analysis. Human Resource Management; Spring, 41, 1: 45 – 66

Luthans, F., D.H.Welsh & Rosenkrantz,S.A. (1993). What do Russian Managers Really Do? An Observational Study with Comparison to US Managers'. Journal of International Business Studies 24/4 : 741-762

Newman, L.K & Nollen, D.S. (1996). Culture and Congruence: The Fit Between Management Practice and National Culture. Journal of International Business Studies. Fourth Quarter, 27, 4: 753 – 779

Pascale, R. T & Maguire, M. A. (1980). Comparison of Selected Work Factors in Japan and The United States. Human Relations, 33: 433-455

Saffold, Guy. (1988). Culture Traits, Strength and Insurance Organizational Performance: Moving Beyond Strong Culture. Academy of Management Review.13,4: 546-558

Schneider, S. C & DeMeyer, A. (1991). Interpreting and Responding to Strategic Issues: The Impact of National Culture. Strategic Management Journal, 12: 307 – 320

Schuler, S Randal & Susan E Jackson. (1996). Human Resource Management. New York: Prentice Hall.

Smith, P. B.(1992). Insurance Organizational Behaviour and National Cultures. British Journal of Management, Vol.3. 39-51

Chin-loy, C., *Assessing the Influence of Insurance Organizational Culture on Knowledge Management*

Success. The Wayne Huizeng School of Business and Entrepreneurship, Nova Southeastern University, UMI Dissertation, 2003

Davenport, T.H and Prusak, L. , *Working Knowledge: How Insurance Organizations Manage What*
They Know, Harvard Business School Press, Boston, 1998
Green, J. , *Cultural awareness in the human services: A multi-ethnic approach,* (2 nd Ed). Toronto: Allyn and Bacon, 1995;
Hodge, BJ, Anthony, WP & Gales, LM, *Insurance Organization theory: a strategic approach*, 5th ed. Prentice Hall, Upper Saddle River, New Jersey, 2002;
Hrop, S.,, *Personnel Psychology*, Volume: 56. Issue: 3, 2003
Robbins, R.F, *Harnessing Group Memory to Build a Knowledge-Sharing Culture*, Of Counsel. Vol. 22, No. 6, pp. 7-11, 2003;
Kotler, Ph., *Kotler on Marketing, How to Create, Win and Dominate Markets*, Simon & Schuster UK Ltd., pp. 3-5 , 2001;
Rogers, E. M., *Diffusion of innovations*, 4th Edition, New York, NY: The Free Press, 1995;
Tanur, J., Jordan B., *Measuring Employee Satisfaction: Corporate surveys as practice*, 1995,
http://www.amstat.org/Sections/Srms/Proceedings/papers/1995_072.pdf
Amah, E (2006) **Human Resource Management**. Amethyst Publishers Port Harcourt.

Baridam, D.M (2001) Research Methods in Adminstrative Sciences. Sherbrooke Associates,
Port Harcourt. 3rd Edition.

Bateman, T.S and Snell, S.A (1999) **Management: Building Competitive Advantage** 4th ed Irwin McGraw Hills Inc. New Jersey

Blenkhorn D.L and Gaber B (1995) "The Useof'WarmFuzzies'to AccessInsurance Organizational
Effectiveness", *Journal of General Management*, 21 No. 2 (winter): 40 – 51.

Bowen D. E and Lawler III, E.E. (1995) "Empowering Service Employees" *Sloan Management Review* (Summer), July 15p 73-84.

Caves, R. E and Porter, M. E (1977) From Entry Business: Conjectural Decisions And Contrived Deterrence to New Competition. *Quarterly Journal of Economics 91:2p241-262*

Child, J. (1974) "Management and Insurance Organizational Factors Associated with Company
Performance – Part I" *Journal of Management Studies*. Vol, II, 3 December pp. 175 –
189.

Child J. (1975) "Managerial and Insurance Organizational Factors Associated with Company
Performance – Part II" *Journal of Management Studies* Vol 12:1-2 pp 12 – 27.
Conger, J.A and Kanugo, R. N (1988) the Empowerment Process: Integrating Theory and Practice," *Academy of Management Review* 13: No. 3. 471-82.
Coye, R. W and Belohlav, J. A (1995) "An Exploratory Analysis of Employee Participation"
Group And Insurance Organization Management 20: N01 pp4-17

Czinkota M.R, Ketabe M and Mercer, D (1997) **Marketing Management**. Blackwell Publishers, Oxford, UK.

Daft, R.L (1998) **Insurance Organization Theory and Design**, 6th Ed, Southwestern College Publishing, Cincinnati, Ohio.

Denison, D.R (1984) 'Bringing Corporate Culture to the Bottom line' *Insurance Organizational Behaviour* 13/2:5 – 22.

Denison, D. R (1985) **Corporate Culture and Insurance Organizational Effectiveness: A Behavioural Approach to Financial Performance**. Wiley-Interscience.

Denison, D.R. (1990) **Corporate Culture and Insurance Organizational Effectiveness**: New York: Wiley.

Denison,D. R (2007) Denison Insurance Organizational Culture Model. Denison Consulting An Arbor Zurich Shanghai

Denison D.R. and Mishra A.K (1995) 'Toward a theory of Insurance Organizational Culture and effectiveness' *Insurance Organization Science* 6: 2 204 – 223.

Ford, R. C and Fottler, M. D (1995) "Empowerment: A Matter of Degree," *Academy of **Management Executive*** **9: 3,p 21-31.**

Friedlander, F and Pickle H. (1968) "Components of Effectiveness in Small Insurance Organizations". *Administrative Science Quarterly* 13: 289 – 304.

Gowen, III, C. R (1990) "Gain Sharing Programs: An Overview of History and Research," *Journal of Insurance Organizational Behavior Management II* (2) pp77-99.

Hall, R.H and Clark, J.P (1980) "An Ineffective Effectiveness Study and Some Suggestions For Future Research," *Sociological Quarterly* 21 No 1 p119-34

Hofstrand, D. (2007) Understanding Profitability. Marketing Resource Centre d.hof@Tastate.edu. June10,2007

Kanungo, S. (1998): An Empirical Study of Insurance Organizational Culture and Network-based Computer Use. *Computers in Human Behaviour*, 14 (1) 79 -91.

Kotler P. (1999) Kotler on Marketing: How to create, win and dominate Markets**. Free Press New York.**

Kotler P and Armstrong G. (2001) **Principles of Marketing** 9th ed. Prentice Hall. NJ USA

Lesieur, F. C, (1958) ed., **The Scanlon Plan: A Frontier in Labour-Management Cooperation**. (Cambridge, M. A: MIT Press).

Liden, R. C and Arad, S (1996) "A Power Perspective of Empowerment and Work groups: Implications for Human Resources Management Research" *Research in Personnel and Human Resources Management* 14: pp 205-51 Greenwich CT: JAI Press.

Likert, R.L (1961) **New Patterns in Management**. N Y McGraw Hill

Luthans, F (1985) Insurance Organization Behaviour 4th Edition (McGraw-Hill, Book Company, Singapore).

Maheshwari, B. I (1980) **Decision Styles and Insurance Organizational Effectiveness**. New Vickas Publishing House. PVT Ltd .Michigan

Mc Caffrey, D. P; Faerman, S. R and Hart, D. W (1995) "The Appeal and Difficulties of Participative Systems," *Insurance Organization Science* 6, no. 6 (November-December): 603-27.

McShane, S.L. and Von Glinow, M.A (2003) **Insurance Organizational Behaviour. Emerging Realities for The Workplace Revolution**. 2nd ed. McGraw Hill Companies Inc. Irwin New York.

Nasar, S (2002) Productivity. The Concise Encyclopedia of Economics. The Library of Economics And Liberty. Accessed at http://www.econlib.org/ June 10 2007

Negandhi, A.R and Reiman B.C (1973) "Task Environment, Decentralization And Insurance Organizational Effectiveness," *Human Relations Journal*. Vol 26 pp203 – 214.

Nickels, G; McHugh, J.M and McHugh, S.M (1997) **Understanding Business**. 4th ed. Irwin McGraw-Hill New York.

Nwachukwu C.C. (2002) **Comparative Management, An Introduction**, Spring Field Publishers Ltd, Owerri Imo State Nigeria.

Nunnally, J. C. (1978). *Psychometric theory* (2nd ed.). New York: McGraw-Hill.

Pennings, J.M and Goodman, P.S (1979) "Toward a workable frame work," in Paul S, Goodman, Johannes M. Pennings, et al, **New Perspectives On Insurance Organizational Effectiveness** (San Francisco : Jossey –Bass).

Porter, M. E (1979) The Structure Within Industries and Companies Performance. *Review of Economic Statistics Vol 61No. 2 pp214 - 262*

Prokopenko, J. (1987) **Productivity Management. A Practical Handbook** Geneva ILO.

Randolph, W.A (2000) "Rethinking Empowerment: Why is it so hard to Achieve?" *Insurance Organizational Dynamics* 29: 2 (November) pp94-107

Rose, F. (1991) "New Quality Means Service Too" *Fortune* April 22; p 99 – 108.

Rossler, P. E and Koelling, C. P (1993) "The Effect of Gain Sharing on Business Performance at a Paper Mill" *National Productivity Review* 12: 3 pp 365-82.

Shipper, F, and Manz, C.C. (1992) "Employee Self Management Without Formally Designated Teams: An Alternative Road to Empowerment" *Insurance Organizational Dynamics* (Winter):3: 48 – 61.

Stewart, T. A (1989) "CEO's See Clout Shifting"Fortune 6 November pp66

Strauss, G (1998) Collective Bargaining, Unions, and Participation, "in F.Heller, E, Pusic, G. Strauss, and B. Wilpert, eds., **Insurance Organizational Participation: Myth and Reality** (New York: Oxford University Press) 97-143

Strasser, S, Eveland, J.D, Cummms, G, Deniston,O.L, and Romani, J.H (1981) "Conceptualizing The Goal and Systems Models of Insurance Organizational Effectiveness – Implications for Comparative Evaluation Research, "*Journal of Management Studies* 18: 321 – 40.

Thompson, A. A and Strickland A.J (2001) Strategic Management: Concepts and Cases 12th ed (Boston: McGraw Hill Irwin).

Vroom, V. H and Jago, A. G (1988) The New Leadership: Managing Participation in Insurance Organizations (Engle wood Cliffs, NJ: Prentice Hall)

Weick, K.E and Daft, R. L (1982) "The Effectiveness of Interpretation Systems," in Kim S.Cameron and David A. Whetten, Eds. Insurance Organizational Effectiveness: A Comparison of Multiple Models (New York: Academic Press).

Weijters, B., Cabooter, E., & Schillewaert, N. (2010). The effect of rating scale format on response styles: The number of response categories and response category labels. International Journal of Research in Marketing, 27, 236-247.

What we do (2015). World Values Survey. Retrieved from: http://www.Worldvaluessurvey.org/WVSContents

Yuan, Y., and Xie, Q. (2011). Cultures of leaming: An evolving concept and an expanding field. In M. Cortazzi and L. Jin (Ed.) Cultures of Learning: International Perspectives on Language Learning and Education (pp. 21-40). New York, NY: Palgrave MacMillan.

www.ingramcontent.com/pod-product-compliance
Lightning Source LLC
LaVergne TN
LVHW060825170826
845678LV00010B/1901

9798372733855